Teaching for
the Lifespan

To two of the most kind and resilient human beings I have ever known:
Mary Jane, my greatest blessing;
Alexia, my dear friend and loving teacher to many children.

—Nicole Ofiesh

To my lifelong friends:
Jim, Scott, and Steve, and to Tom, who died
too soon but still keeps me laughing.

—Henry Reiff

Teaching for the Lifespan

*Successfully Transitioning Students
With Learning Differences to Adulthood*

Henry B. Reiff
Nicole S. Ofiesh

CORWIN
A SAGE Company

FOR INFORMATION:

Corwin

A SAGE Company

2455 Teller Road

Thousand Oaks, California 91320

(800) 233-9936

www.corwin.com

SAGE Publications Ltd.

1 Oliver's Yard

55 City Road

London EC1Y 1SP

United Kingdom

SAGE Publications India Pvt. Ltd.

B 1/I 1 Mohan Cooperative Industrial Area

Mathura Road, New Delhi 110 044

India

SAGE Publications Asia-Pacific Pte. Ltd.

3 Church Street

#10-04 Samsung Hub

Singapore 049483

Acquisition Editor: Jessica Allan

Associate Editor: Kimberly Greenberg

Editorial Assistant: Katie Crilley

Production Editor: Amy Schroller

Copy Editor: Erin Livingston

Typesetter: C&M Digitals (P) Ltd.

Proofreader: Dennis W. Webb

Indexer: Terri Morrissey

Cover Designer: Alexa Turner

Marketing Manager: Jill Margulies

Printed in the United States of America

ISBN 978-1-4833-7384-3

This book is printed on acid-free paper.

SFI° Certified Sourcing
www.sfiprogram.org
SFI-00453

15 16 17 18 19 10 9 8 7 6 5 4 3 2 1

Contents

Foreword

I was pleased to be asked to write the foreword for what promises to be a most important and valuable book. The authors have quite properly taken on a large and demanding task—focusing on ways to prepare students with varied learning differences for success in school as well as in their lives after school.

Too often, and for too long, teachers and educational researchers, with the best of intentions, have focused almost exclusively on traditional academic skills and capabilities. The basic academic program and criteria have been seen as a given, never to be challenged or rethought. They have seen their job as fixing what is wrong within a narrow traditional academic focus.

Often, educators have ignored the obvious reality that there are many facets of work and life that have little to do with traditional school subjects—or with conforming to traditional school-oriented tests and measurements of ability. Those of us who have taken a long look at individuals with dyslexia and other learning differences are painfully aware of the great potential for moderate success, or sometimes very high success, for these individuals in technological innovation, art and design creativity, scientific discovery, and entrepreneurial business.

By definition, individuals with learning differences may have great difficulties in some areas, but they may also have distinctive capabilities and talents that are valuable in life and work, although these may be largely ignored during the school years. These issues are increasingly important in a time of profound change, as digital technologies transform what is desired in the workplace and how these capabilities are being measured.

Educators who remain focused on the old world of words and numbers, memorization, and rapid recall risk missing how much has already changed in the new world of computer images and information visualization, where pattern recognition and true design innovation now largely drive corporate success or scientific discovery. Many have obsessed over building 19th-century capabilities when 21st-century capabilities have been largely ignored, remaining undefined and undeveloped.

I am grateful to Drs. Henry Reiff and Nicole Ofiesh for casting their light on these new realities and the things we need to do in this very different new world. For example, they quite properly focus on a paradigm shift toward a strengths-based model of education. They acknowledge the deep and pervasive role of the newest technological trends. They argue that new instructional approaches should be designed to benefit all students, not just a few. And they draw our attention to the persistent problem of whether students should be taught to own a label that is not well understood by the outside world.

Learning differences can take many forms, but the history of one of the most common—developmental dyslexia—is broadly instructive. From the time of the earliest researchers (in the 1890s) to Samuel Torrey Orton (in the 1920s) and Norman Geschwind (in the 1980s), the central puzzle of developmental dyslexia has always been the linkage of high ability in some areas with remarkable and unexpected difficulties and disabilities in other areas.

For more than a century, we have recognized this pattern but have generally focused on only one aspect. With the best of intentions, we have learned much about how to fix the problems that people with learning differences experience, but we have done almost nothing to develop a deeper and systematic understanding of the varied and hard-to-measure talents that they possess.

An increasing number of us have come to believe that learning from the lives of successful individuals with dyslexia and learning differences can lead to new insights and approaches that will help all students, profoundly transforming fundamental ideas about education and work at a time when computer technologies have turned the world upside down and many of the established professionals seem to have lost their way.

It is high time for us to begin to recognize and understand and learn how to deal with these puzzling extremes in talent—the unexpected academic weaknesses that often seem to be associated with special capabilities and success in both life and work. Low-level weaknesses should not be allowed to prevent high-level accomplishment. Schools almost never teach or test what these students are good at, but life does.

Highly successful dyslexics nearly always say that their accomplishments and special ways of seeing come directly from, not in spite of, their dyslexia. We should take them at their word and give credence to what they say. Most conventional researchers and professionals have long agreed that talents are important. However, eventually, they almost always come to focus exclusively on the near-term problems of academic remediation alone. We hope this will change.

In a time with many future uncertainties, it seems that we badly need the big-picture thinking and original insights that seem to be the signature contributions of the most successful individuals with learning differences. It is a paradox among many paradoxes, but it may be that those who would appear initially to need the most help could, in time, be those most likely to be able to help the most.

Thomas G. West
Author of *In the Mind's Eye*
and *Thinking Like Einstein*
Washington, DC, May 2015

Acknowledgments

We would like to thank Jessica Allan and the amazing staff at Corwin for their support and assistance in the development of our work.

About the Authors

Henry B. Reiff is a writer, public speaker, researcher, and leader in the field of learning differences and the community. He has published numerous articles on adults and adolescents with learning differences and has written or cowritten four books, including *Exceeding Expectations: Successful Adults With Learning Disabilities*, an American Library Association Top 20 LD Resource. His most recent book is *Self-Advocacy for Students With Learning Disabilities: Making It Happen in College and Beyond*. He has given presentations and workshops across the country. Currently a regular blogger on the popular website, *Friends of Quinn*, Dr. Reiff continues to focus on promoting positive outcomes for persons with learning differences.

A faculty member in special education at McDaniel College since 1989, Dr. Reiff has served as dean of student academic life and dean of graduate and professional studies for 19 of those years. He is currently professor of education and coordinator of the graduate program in special education at McDaniel. He regularly counsels young adults with learning differences. He and his wife, Jacki, reside in Westminster, MD, with their two children and two dogs.

Nicole S. Ofiesh is an internationally recognized expert in the field of learning and assessment. Her experiences are diverse and span over thirty years. In her roles as a learning specialist, teacher educator, researcher, speaker, author, and consultant, she works with children, adolescents, and adults. Her work has kept her passionate about creating positive and valid educational experiences!

Dr. Ofiesh has held faculty positions at Providence College, Notre Dame de Namur University, and the University of Arizona, and she currently conducts research at Stanford University.

Dr. Ofiesh's work is dedicated to the development of assessment systems that allow all individuals to learn and to demonstrate knowledge in order to maximize performance. She regularly consults with corporations, clinics, and schools (from elementary through graduate school) on program design and professional development. She has served as an expert to the United States Department of Justice, Office of Civil Rights, and large-scale test organizations on testing and persons with disabilities.

At the heart of her work is the belief that individuals should *thrive*, not simply survive. She centers her work on research on the human condition, resilience, cognition, performance, and technology. Dr. Ofiesh began to work with children with emotional and behavioral disorders in 1985 in San Francisco. Many of these children were in and out of prison. It was there that she became familiar with the educational system in the United States and how successful learning experiences can change a person's life. After returning to San Francisco State University for a master's degree in learning disabilities, teaching credential, and an educational therapy certificate, she continued to work as a learning specialist with children and adults. She completed her doctoral program at Penn State University in 1997 with an emphasis on transition and postsecondary education for individuals with disabilities. She is a Fellow of the International Academy for Research in Learning Disabilities and author of numerous research articles and book chapters.

Introduction

"How can I best help my students with learning differences lead satisfying and meaningful adult lives?" Trying to answer the question is the purpose of this book. The undertaking is maddeningly complex. It requires building perspectives from multiple contexts and applying them in an infinite array of individual interactions. This process may challenge attitudes, alter belief systems, and catalyze innovative approaches to teaching and learning. Teachers who aspire to prepare students with learning differences for a satisfying adulthood are those who embrace teaching as "the hardest job you'll ever love."

Teachers and parents need to understand the journey that takes individuals to adulthood. They need to acquire dispositions and pedagogical practices that prioritize promoting the strengths and abilities of people with learning differences as opposed to fixing weaknesses and limitations. Helping students with learning differences develop an awareness of proactive behaviors increases the likelihood of both vocational success and overall positive adaptation to the demands of adult life. Many children with learning differences grow up to be highly successful adults who often share how they managed to "turn the lemon into lemonade," as one individual described his journey. Students who acquire specific skills that adults with learning differences have used to be successful are truly preparing for adulthood. This book is about teaching for the lifespan.

We have worked with many teachers over the years who focus on strengths rather than weaknesses. They embrace the whole student. They understand that traditional academics do not always provide a foundation for negotiating the complexities of the adult world. These teachers find innovative ways to prepare students for the rest of their lives. We believe that a broad knowledge base of learning differences, adult development theory, and perspectives on success may contribute significantly to teaching effectiveness. This book will help teachers by providing the foundation for understanding the nature of adulthood of individuals with learning differences.

We have also worked with teachers who do not welcome such a holistic approach. Many are dedicated but limit their focus to traditional academic disciplines and rigid pedagogical methods. Unfortunately, some seem not to care deeply about building positive foundations. Another goal of this book is for readers willingly to take on the roles of change agents who help others consider alternate ideas about education.

What happens to kids with learning differences when they grow up? The general public still questions whether learning differences simply go away once students have exited school. Learning disabilities (and many other learning differences) are traditionally school-based deficits, generally diagnosed in school. Even now, students with learning differences are often tempted to leave their learning differences behind. Many believe their learning differences will not have an impact in college, work, relationships, and, especially, feelings about themselves.

Learning differences do not end once students have finished school. The adult world is certainly different from the school environment. Adults with learning differences are not routinely assessed, evaluated, and judged by teachers, nor do they bear the public educational labels of their schooling. Yet the same difficulties with processing information persist, except they manifest themselves in different ways. Adults with difficulties with reading, writing, or math do not flunk tests, but these problems still affect work and personal life. Knowledge about adult outcomes for persons with learning differences presents an important perspective for teaching and parenting children.

Explicit techniques based on understanding individual learning styles can prepare students for the rest of their lives. Some of these techniques are routinely part of special education pedagogy and represent commonsense notions of good teaching. Others are innovative and ask us to think outside the box. Individualized instruction, multimodality approaches, multisensory approaches, and an intentional effort to know and understand each student should be in the repertoire of all teachers.

Part I of the book offers a multidimensional context for understanding learning differences in adulthood. Part II takes established best practices as well as current models and shows how teachers may use them to prepare their students for the lifespan. Few things feel better than seeing your students and children succeed years after they have finished school and left home. So, let's get started on successfully transitioning students with learning differences to adulthood.

PART I

Context

For in every adult there dwells the child that was, and in every child there lies the adult that will be.

—John Connolly, *The Book of Lost Things*

Several areas of research contribute to the approaches described in this book. In Part I, we devote a chapter to each of these areas. A glance at these chapter titles emphasizes our belief that as teachers, parents, and pertinent role models, we must enter the classroom with the awareness that we are teaching each child for a lifetime. Therefore, we ground our context within research and theory on (1) the construct of learning differences, (2) adult developmental theory and individuals with learning differences, (3) keys to success, and (4) successes and outcomes of adults with learning differences, with a focus on their application for both students and adults with learning differences. Theory and empirical evidence of best practices provide the foundation to help us increase the likelihood of satisfying adult outcomes for students with learning differences.

1 The Construct of Learning Differences

Attitudes are the real disability.

—Henry Holden

How do we view the notion of disability? Most of us take the term for granted, but how is it relevant to persons with *learning differences*, a term not used in the law, research, or diagnostic manuals? Ultimately, we want our children to enter into adulthood with self-awareness and personal autonomy. Identifying people with learning differences as disabled influences the way we perceive and act toward them and the way they perceive themselves. The story of why we call children who learn differently *disabled* comes from many different areas. The term *disability* is more than a medical, psychological, or educational issue; it has roots in politics, economics, and our culture. If we desire to empower students who learn differently to succeed in life, we need to understand how we came to our current place of identifying and teaching students with learning differences as learning disabled.

A FUNDAMENTAL QUESTION

It is critical to begin any discussion of working with students who learn differently by addressing two fundamental questions for all teachers, parents, and students themselves: What do we mean by learning *differences*? How are they similar to and different from learning *disabilities*? As teachers know, students take on all shapes and forms. Our use of the term *learning differences*, first and foremost, is intended to represent the spectrum of individuals who have the ability to live independently and who learn differently. The term *learning disability* traditionally refers to individuals who, in spite of their average to gifted abilities and a potential to learn, have difficulties meeting expectations of achievement, particularly in a school setting. They have difficulty learning how to read, write, or do mathematical calculations as well as carry out executive functions and other skills. The atypical challenges these children and adults face every day are not readily noticed by others the way one may notice a person with blindness who uses a cane or a person who uses a wheelchair. In this regard, the disability is hidden or invisible. Therefore, unlike disabilities that are diagnosed soon after birth, the presence of a learning disability may not be recognized until the academic demands of a general education classroom become inordinately hard to attain without additional support. These students need the support because they learn *differently*.

Many eventually are diagnosed and identified with a specific label. Students with these diagnoses typically learn and demonstrate their knowledge differently to such a significant level that they are identified as having a disability (most commonly under the categories of Specific Learning Disability, Speech and Language Disorder, or Other Health Impaired) under the Individuals with Disabilities Education Improvement Act (IDEA) of 2004. In our educational system, labels play an important role; the use of the term *disability* is needed in order to qualify for the services offered in an Individual Education Program (IEP) and other services. However, for a variety of reasons, many students who learn differently do not meet specific eligibility requirements to be identified as having a disability. For these individuals, support may be withheld, at the child's expense. We question the fairness of withholding services for students with learning differences who do not meet eligibility criteria as disabled but certainly deserve special support. Because the intention of this book is to address the needs of a wide range of students with mild to moderate learning needs as well as those who are ineligible for services but who indeed learn differently, we use the term *learning differences*.

A PARADIGM SHIFT TO A STRENGTHS-BASED MODEL

We prefer to use the term *learning differences* rather than *learning disabilities* because of the meanings commonly associated with the latter label by many outside of special education. Many laypersons lack knowledge about learning disabilities and believe that a learning disability and developmental delay are synonymous. Because of the invisible nature of cognition, some might think that these students are lazy or unmotivated or that their parents have false expectations of success for them. In some instances there may also be a perception that these students and their parents are gaming the system to receive accommodations on high-stakes tests that will provide a competitive edge on college entrance requirements. All of these assumptions about individuals with learning differences are false. We must ask ourselves what the benefits are of teaching children to own a label of disability that is not accepted or readily understood by the general public and even many teachers. Diagnoses of disorders that are traditionally school-based deficits are generally diagnosed before college. Therefore, over time, some students with learning differences are often tempted to leave their label of *disabled* behind. Many believe their learning differences will not have an impact in college, work, relationships, and, especially, feelings about themselves. Many do not want to be associated with a label that has made them feel less than adequate. By minimizing the term *disability* and broadening our scope to *learning differences*, we believe we promote the transition to a new era of education. While doing so, however, we still believe in the continuum of services, accommodations, and settings that must be allowed for all individuals who are eligible for special education.

We are at a crossroads in education where access to instruction through technology, the Common Core State Standards (CCSS), and Universal Design for Learning (UDL) suggest we change our notion of disability to one of differences. Doing so allows most children to learn successfully in general education classrooms and to learn more effectively in resource rooms. Technology is changing the very way we see the world, each other, and ourselves. It is rapidly breaking down barriers that have thwarted the progress of untold numbers of students with learning differences. The CCSS offer opportunities to minimize the separateness of students with learning differences. It encourages students with learning differences to take on the academic content standards formerly reserved for students without disabilities. The UDL framework minimizes the concept of disabilities in the classroom. It emphasizes instructional approaches that work for all students instead of a traditional model that compartmentalizes instruction into two categories: traditional approaches for "normal" students and special approaches for students with disabilities. In short, UDL levels the playing field. It counters the marginalization of students with learning disabilities and other labels. We all learn differently to one degree or another and have learning preferences that are invariably our learning strengths. As we embrace UDL as part of the CCSS, there is a need to minimize the relevance of categorical distinctions and emphasize learning strengths.

CCSS and Students With Learning Differences

Margaret J. McLaughlin, the associate dean for research and graduate education at the University of Maryland and former president of the Council for Exceptional Children (CEC), believes that implementation of the CCSS can inclusively respond to the unique and varied learning needs of students with learning differences. She recommends a number of practices to help support students with disabilities and create an inclusive environment where differences rather than disabilities will drive instruction and assessment. We have extracted the following nuggets of wisdom and blended them with some of our ideas but recommend checking out the full article (http://www.naesp.org/principal-septemberoctober-2012-common-core/access-common-core-all-0).

- Teachers must recognize that every student with learning differences is unique and needs an individualized approach.
- UDL is the best way to accomplish the goals of providing multiple means for all students to learn within their individual needs.
- We know of methods that work (i.e., best practices). Use them!
- Teachers and the administration should find ways to monitor student progress toward meeting CCSS throughout the year and not rely exclusively on once-per-year high-stakes testing.
- Goals on IEPs can and should be aligned with CCSS.
- We need the best teachers we can find. School systems that invest in high-quality teachers will serve students with learning differences (and all students) well.

Rather than try to change the way students with learning disabilities learn, we are beginning to change environments so that all students can learn. If students who have failed in traditional educational settings subsequently find success in different ones, what is the relevance of the label *learning disabilities*? We have the opportunity to shift to a more positive strengths-based model by providing teachers with a multitude of ways to allow children and young adults to experience education. Although learning differences make learning exceedingly difficult in specific ways, these students have strengths in areas typically not noticed in school. These include visualization, analytical thinking, analogous thinking, awareness of the environment, and narrative thinking. Use of the term *learning differences* allows us to adopt a strengths-based model that embraces the whole child.

HISTORICAL PERSPECTIVES

In order to build a better context for our understanding of learning differences, a quick look at the history of the field of learning disabilities provides valuable insights. Even though the realization that some people learn differently and do better with specialized instruction took root in the 1930s, schools did not offer mandated services until 1975. Even by that time, learning disabilities were best conceptualized by what they are not rather than by what they are.

DEFINITIONS OF LEARNING DISABILITIES: HOW MUCH DO THEY MATTER?

The timeline of learning disabilities leads to a somewhat bizarre conclusion. After a century of exploring the issues of children who learn differently, a lack of consensus persists on the very nature of learning disabilities. Hammill (1990) wrote about the eleven most common definitions of learning disabilities. No one agrees on what they are. The federal definition drives evaluation and identification of learning disabilities (Specific Learning Disabilities, U.S. Office of Education, 1977). It includes

- a disorder in one or more of the basic psychological processes,
- perceptual handicaps, brain injury, minimal brain dysfunction, dyslexia, and developmental aphasia; and
- excludes children who have learning disabilities which are primarily the result of visual, hearing, or motor handicaps, or mental retardation, or emotional disturbance, or of environmental, cultural, or economic disadvantage.

A Brief (and Incomplete) Timeline of the History of Learning Disabilities

- 1917: James Hinshelwood, MD, popularizes the term *word blindness* to describe some of his patients who, in spite of normal visual acuity and intelligence, had significant difficulties reading.
- 1920s and 1930s: Samuel Orton terms this reading condition *strephosymbolia*, derived from his observation that many of the children he studied made reversals or transpositions despite average or above-average scores on the Stanford-Binet IQ test. The phenomenon is commonly referred to as *dyslexia*.
- 1940s and 1950s: Alfred Strauss, Heinz Werner, and Laura Lehtinen's work with brain-injured soldiers results in Strauss Syndrome: abnormal responses to environmental stimuli, distractibility, perseveration, higher levels of motor activity, hyperactivity, disorganized behavior, perceptual disturbances, and motor problems.
- 1963: Samuel Kirk proposes the term *learning disabilities* to describe children with reading and other difficulties, based on theories of minimal brain dysfunction and perceptual-motor deficits.
- 1970s to present: A lack of consensus continues on the definition of learning disabilities. The majority of learning differences do not conform to the educational criteria of diagnosis and subsequent services.
- 1993: Mel Levine and others conclude that definitions of learning disabilities are vague, describing what a learning disability is not rather than what it is.
- 2000s to present: Controversy over assessment and eligibility for special education increases with the development of Response to Intervention (RTI) models. The validity of the construct of learning disability is attacked and successfully defended by researchers, advocates, and the National Joint Committee on Learning Disabilities (NJCLD, 1991).

The IDEA 2004 guidance governs identification of students who have a severe discrepancy between achievement and intellectual ability or who do not show a response to structured interventions as having learning disabilities. The documentation of the discrepancy in the model usually involves a comparison of some kind of test of cognitive ability (usually the Woodcock Johnson Tests of Cognitive Ability-IV or one of the Wechsler Intelligence scales) with tests of achievement (e.g., Woodcock Johnson Tests of Achievement-IV, Stanford Achievement Tests, Wechsler Individual Achievement Test-III, or Kaufman Test of Educational Achievement-II).

The discrepancy issue is controversial if not contentious and, in recent years, has fallen out of favor as a requirement for special education services for individuals with specific learning disabilities. The conjecture that a discrepancy between aptitude and achievement constitutes a learning disability is just that—a conjecture. The aptitude-achievement discrepancy model was an attempt to operationally define how big the discrepancy must be in order for a student to qualify for special education services under the category of Specific Learning Disability. It has been widely misapplied, and little attention was ever paid to the laws that allowed a school district to professionally qualify a student based on need, even if the discrepancy was not met (Ofiesh, 2006). Consequently, states use different criteria for determining what constitutes a "significant" discrepancy, meaning that a child may have learning disabilities in one state but not another. Those who qualify typically receive an IEP. Some others labeled as emotionally disturbed or who have intellectual deficits also qualify for the IEP or 504 plan. Most other students with significant learning difficulties do not have an IEP and do not receive the learning support, remediation, and accommodations that go with it. Their testing does not reveal enough of a discrepancy between ability and achievement. They are not failing *enough*. The need to fail smacks of educational and social injustice.

A second problem with the aptitude-achievement discrepancy is that too frequently a critical aspect of the construct of a learning disability is ignored: a disorder in one or more basic psychological processes. This disorder in a basic psychological process (e.g., oral language ability vs. rapid naming ability) is at the root of the learning disability and helps to illuminate why the individual is struggling in math, for example. Many diagnosticians overlook this important aspect of the federal definition and instead devote much of the evaluation to calculating the discrepancy between aptitude and achievement.

This reality gives a compelling argument for the use of *learning differences* rather than *learning disabilities*. The category of Specific Learning Disability excludes countless students with significant learning differences who do not meet eligibility criteria. These students may get some support through what is called a 504 plan, but many do not get the support that could make a significant difference in their educational outcomes. Rather than getting hung up on a label, we should focus on the much broader array of students with learning differences. They too need accommodations, instructional adjustments, clear learning goals, and meaningful assessment.

From our perspective, the NJCLD offers a definition that describes this phenomenon and postulates reasons for it. A number of different perspectives inform this definition of *disabilities*. Here are the major points:

- Uses a general term that refers to a heterogeneous group of disorders: significant difficulties in the acquisition and use of listening, speaking, reading, writing, reasoning, or mathematical abilities
- Is intrinsic to the individual
- Presumes central nervous system dysfunction
- Occurs across lifespan
- Acknowledges that problems with social perception and social interaction may exist with learning disabilities but do not by themselves constitute a learning disability
- Excludes children who have learning difficulties due primarily to other disabilities or cultural differences or insufficient or inappropriate instruction. (NJCLD, 1991)

The first part of this definition is noteworthy: The first thing to know about learning disabilities is that it is a "general term" and a "heterogeneous group of disorders" (p. 20). To break this down into the vernacular, *learning disabilities* is a general way of cataloguing almost *all* the kinds of difficulties people can have with learning! Consequently, it is a matter of some debate whether these difficulties are truly disabilities or rather part of the overall spectrum of human differences.

The NJCLD definition does include several tenets that try to give more specificity, particularly the attention to the disorders being "intrinsic to the individual, presumed to be due to central nervous system dysfunction" (p. 20). Essentially, this phrase indicates that children are born with their particular learning styles. At some level, their brains are hardwired to process information differently than many or most of us. The majority of persons with learning differences, whether diagnosed or not, will tell you that they have been this way as long as they can remember. Their distinct ways of approaching tasks, learning, and the world are more rooted in nature than the environment. They will also tell you that their learning differences persist through adulthood.

As with most definitions, it does a better job of explaining what learning disabilities are *not*. "Problems in self-regulatory behaviors, social perception, and social interaction may exist with learning disabilities but do not by themselves constitute a learning disability" (p. 20). *Self-regulatory behaviors* describe attention deficit/hyperactivity disorder (ADHD). A debate within the committee ensued regarding whether ADHD should be included in the definition. This rather technical distinction resulted from both social and theoretical ideologies. Whatever the objection, distractibility, inattentiveness, and inattention have a pronounced negative effect on learning and achievement. Students with ADHD who qualify for an IEP fall under the category of Other Health Impaired.

The professional community in the field of learning disabilities has recognized the term *nonverbal learning disabilities* (NVLD). Representing the National Center for Learning Disabilities on its website (http://www.ncld .org), Sheldon H. Horowitz, EdD describes the characteristics of NVLD as including difficulties with understanding social nuances such as sarcasm or how to ingratiate into a conversation, general social awkwardness, and incessant talking. Many of these behaviors reflect a seeming social obliviousness.

From our perspective, NVLD are learning differences. Understanding the social world of human interactions is the basis for functioning effectively in our environment, which includes achieving in the classroom environment. Lending credence to this observation, the Learning Disabilities Association (LDA), formerly the Association for Children with Learning Disabilities (ACLD), incorporates social perception as a primary characteristic in its definition (ACLD, 1986).

Many K–12 educators do not see social perception and nonverbal language as part of the curriculum or their teaching responsibilities. However, more and children struggle with what is known as the *hidden curriculum*, the complex system of rules and behavioral expectations of school culture, because of these difficulties (Giddens, 1972). It is often up to parents and well-informed teachers to implement social skills or language development training in schools. Many programs are available. We will review a number of these in Part II of this book.

Countless children and adults go undiagnosed. In some cases, they do not have sufficient advocacy to request testing, lack the resources to get tested, or are dismissed as simply underachieving because of skin color, ethnicity, or English as a second language. A recent conference on dyslexia and minorities revealed an overwhelming number of children of color who are untested and undiagnosed (Bowen, 2013). Fair and accessible assessment is an issue of civil rights; barriers to receiving accommodations and services cause a kind of double marginalization for minority children. Later on in life, many of these young adults must pay for costly diagnostic evaluations to substantiate a request for accommodations on tests standardized college admissions tests or professional licensing exams. Some must settle for unaccommodated test scores that do not reflect their true skills and knowledge because they cannot afford the documentation, perpetuating a cycle of discrimination and lack of opportunity.

Increasingly, the RTI model or Multi-Tiered System of Support (MTSS) for determining whether learning disabilities exist has gained favor in research and, to a lesser degree, practice. Formerly, students who were suspected of having learning disabilities went through a cursory screening followed by testing for diagnosis with the ability-achievement discrepancy model. RTI places much greater importance on systematically trying different modes of instruction. Many students with learning differences do better when teachers find ways of meeting their individual learning styles with research-based instruction. RTI reduces the traditional reliance on testing and evaluation, is available to greater numbers of students, and increases the opportunities for students with learning differences to succeed. While RTI holds significant hope for early intervention, it should not be used to determine eligibility for services under an IEP. Without diagnostic testing that allows us to truly understand an individual's strengths and needs, individuals with learning disabilities may never understand their learning differences as well as their strengths (Ofiesh, 2006).

DIFFERENCES, NOT DISABILITIES

Disability is the fundamental term and the bedrock of the philosophies, policies, and practices embedded in the IDEA. The concept greatly influences political, social, economic, and cultural systems. It owes much to the field of abnormal psychology as well as social Darwinism and general intolerance of anything that does not conform to traditional beliefs and economic productivity.

This philosophy distorts the "survival of the fittest" axiom from the theory of evolution and applies it to our social interactions, expectations, and opportunities. In social Darwinism, those who are successful have achieved because they are strong; those who do not are weak. In fact, their weaknesses doom them to extinction. People who fit this category deserve to be marginalized because they do not contribute. They are inferior and often labeled as disabled. Sometimes it is obvious why they are labeled as weak or inferior: They are blind or deaf or have physical limitations.

From the beginning of human history, being able to see, hear, or walk was critical to survival. Vulnerability was disability. Physical and sensory disabilities were (and are) obvious. As the need for a literate and educated populace has increased, we have now deemed problems with literacy and learning as a detriment to social progress—and hence as disabilities. Disabilities have arisen as the needs of society have changed. We test shortcomings in terms of IQ or learning or social behavior to tell us whether someone, particularly a student, is weak or inferior.

In order to decide what is abnormal, we need to define what is normal. Psychologists have a way to do this, interestingly rooted in the work of Francis Galton, a cousin of Darwin himself. Galton noticed that on virtually any human characteristic, about two thirds of the population were pretty similar to each other, but as the characteristic became either greater or smaller (e.g., height, weight, athletic ability), the numbers started to drop dramatically. Only a small number of the population wound up at the extreme end or *tail* of the distribution. This phenomenon resulted in the creation of the *bell curve* or normal distribution. Psychologists found that when they measured attributes such as intelligence, the same distribution occurred. When they used the mean score and then calculated the average variation (or *standard deviation*) from the mean, they found that about two thirds of the persons taking the test scored within this range. The most common score was the mean or close to it, with progressively fewer people getting scores that deviated from the mean. The 68% of the population who scored within one standard deviation were considered *normal* or *average*; the 14% within the next deviation both above and below the mean (a total of 28%) were called *high average* and *low average* respectively; and the remaining 2% on either end were called *abnormal*. It is still a bit of an inside joke to say, "That dude is more than two standard deviations off the mean."

Consequently, we have a statistical definition or construct of disability. That is, a *disability* means being in the bottom 2%, particularly on measures such as intelligence tests. (The top 2% are *gifted*.) Psychologists can measure all sorts of human traits, such as social/emotional and behavioral functioning. In each case, they determine a norm and what is two standard deviations below the norm.

Statistically determining a disability rests on the validity of the tests used to measure different human qualities. Let's start with IQ testing. Do we agree on or even understand what *intelligence* means? If we could come to a consensus on what intelligence means and what kinds of questions we should ask to measure it, do those questions truly represent our construct? Even if the answer is yes, do our different backgrounds have an effect on how we might answer the questions? Do we know whether the number we come up with is an accurate representation of someone's intelligence? School psychologists are taught that there is standard error of measurement with which to view one particular score. Are there other variables that might affect the score? If one looks at the various models of intelligence and abilities (e.g., Cattell-Horn-Carroll, Kaufman, Sternberg, Wechsler), we can see that there is no one clear global construct of intelligence. We can, however, statistically validate what is normal and what is not—at least, on certain attributes. Most individuals will have strengths and weaknesses but not as pronounced as they are in individuals with learning differences. However, many—if not all—of us wind up in the bottom 2% (or close to it) on something. There is a bottom 2% of husbands who lack mechanical aptitude. Two out of a hundred people rank at the bottom in terms of musical or artistic ability. We do not define persons as disabled if their particular weakness does not

> ### Henry's Story
>
> When I teach an introductory special education course, students often ask a panel of deaf adults, "Don't you wish you could hear?" The students are always amazed when they hear, "No, because this is who I am and I cannot imagine being a different person." They cannot hear, but so what? They value their quality of life as well as a heightened awareness of other senses. To what extent is disability in the eye of the beholder? If an individual rejects the label of disability, we need to respect that decision. This is the core of personal autonomy. Everyone wants to feel empowered through a positive sense of self-identity.

"substantially limit one or more major life activities." This is the wording from the Americans with Disabilities Act (ADA). The federal government decides what constitutes a major life activity. School is considered to be a major life activity. (Some still argue that testing is a major life activity.) As much as we may think we agree on what major life activities are (e.g., education, vocation, communication, independence), why *do* we agree— and do we always agree? This is where the notion of disability becomes a social and cultural construct. While not entirely arbitrary, major life activities are what society deems as important. In education, the 3Rs are important; music and art, not so much. A very successful artist with "learning disabilities" once told us, "If some people can't read or write or do mathematics but they can do art, they're learning disabled. But what about the people who can't do art or music, what are they labeled? They're not labeled anything."

The deaf community, in particular, has rejected the notion of disability. They do not have disabilities; they simply are people who use a different language than that of hearing people to communicate. Those of us who do not know sign language may have a disability in the eyes of deaf persons.

Why do we assume persons with disabilities should try to be somebody different? The "something's wrong/fix it" approach is based on an assumption that people with disabilities would prefer not to have disabilities. While this may be true in some cases, our experience has indicated quite the opposite. Ask yourself, "Do I want to be different from who I am at my very essence?" A central component of healthy self-autonomy is satisfaction and belief in oneself. As Beauchamp and Childress state,

> The core idea of personal autonomy is to have personal rule of the self while remaining free from controlling interference by others. The autonomous person acts in accordance with a freely self-chosen and informed plan. A person of diminished autonomy, by contrast, is in at least some respects controlled by others or is incapable of deliberating or acting on the basis of his or her own plans. For example, institutionalized persons, such as prisoners or the mentally retarded, may have diminished autonomy. (1989, p. 68)

Perhaps, as humans, we are innately disposed to fear and reject anything that is different. In many cases, we assuage our wariness of differences by calling them disabilities. It is a convenient way to marginalize those who do not quite fit our expectations of normal behavior. They may not have the same abilities or characteristics as the rest of us (although one has to wonder what attributes define us as being the same as each other), but we overstep when we classify those abilities as *dis-*: "a Latin prefix meaning 'apart,' 'asunder,' 'away,' 'utterly,' or having a privative, negative, or reversing force" (Random House Online Dictionary, 2013). The connotation of "negative" particularly stands out. An adult with profound dyslexia once said, "I went through a time where they were calling kids like me 'mentally retarded.' I don't even know what the other names were but they all came out being subhuman" (Reiff, Gerber, & Ginsberg, 1997). This individual, John Corcoran, is a multimillionaire contractor/developer who has been the subject of innumerable articles in prominent media and is a respected speaker on dyslexia.

The premise that disabilities are a weakness has led to a medical pathology model. The presumption that something is wrong with people that needs to be fixed or cured has a ring of arrogance and condescension. Disabilities represent diversity and differences along the continuum of human beings. Conceptualizing them as *deficient* brings us back to the stigma that many in education and human service professions have been challenging and fighting for years.

Identifying a learning disability can be laborious. The process usually involves filling out a vast amount of paperwork and waiting sometimes over a year for testing to occur. Then, detailed results are shared with teachers and parents. The report usually includes various generic strategies for helping the student be more successful in the classroom—not necessarily to maximize learning potential. The report leads to the creation of an IEP and more paperwork and meetings. Meanwhile, the student is left feeling disabled solely because she or he doesn't fit the traditional school structures and processes that haven't really changed for years. We sometimes overdiagnose and pin on labels as if we have some educational MRI. Plenty of students process information differently to a point that it becomes a functional problem. If it is a problem, teachers should *want* to deal with it. Students with learning differences do not need to be "diagnosed" with a disability.

MOVING FORWARD

Almost 20 years ago, Pat Wolfe wrote about what we know from brain research that can be applied to education. At the time, the idea that IQ is not fixed at birth and that the brain develops over time in relation to the environment was groundbreaking and should have had significant impact on how we teach children in our schools. Wolfe continues her work today through Mind Matters.

Others working to bring brain research into our classrooms include Sarah-Jayne Blackmore and Uta Frith, authors of *The Learning Brain: Lessons for Education*, and Eric Jensen, author of *Teaching With the Brain in Mind*. Even though their work should be game changing and impact core content in teacher training and professional development programs, it has not been sufficiently linked to educational policy and practice. Also over twenty years

The Bottom Line

Carol Hunter, an award-winning retired elementary school principal, is the author of *Real Leadership Real Change* and president of Impact Leadership, a consulting company focused on bringing real change to public education. She articulately expresses a bottom line on the use of the learning disabilities label:

> For those who are comforted by labels and the certainty they provide, it is difficult to embrace the idea that we can unlock the potential of many of our students by determining how they learn. Once we decide that many diagnosed learning disabilities refer to having trouble in a school-based learning environment, we can move forward with defining individual learning styles, brain strengths and intelligences.

Carol also explains her viewpoint in more detail:

> When I first became a principal in 1980, I was exposed to the work of Rita Dunne in the area of learning styles. Fortunately, I was working in a school system that truly empowered principals and teachers to do whatever it took to reach their students. In the site-based management model, the staff and community worked together to determine budget priorities, school organization, and programming. Rita Dunne's work that defined twenty-one elements of learning styles altered classroom practices accordingly. Students were allowed to listen to music, move around the classroom, doodle or fiddle during a lesson, eat while learning, choose more comfortable seating, and so on. Chaos did not reign. Teachers knew which of the twenty-one elements were significant for each child and guided them to choose accordingly. Results were incredible. Unfortunately, the current nod to learning styles focuses almost exclusively on visual, auditory, and kinesthetic learning—all necessary, but not sufficient.

ago, David Rose, the founder of the Center for Applied Special Technology, used brain research to apply universal design to education in his paradigm, UDL.

In 1983, Howard Gardner published *Frames of Mind: The Theory of Multiple Intelligences*. At that time, he identified seven intelligences: linguistic, logic-mathematical, musical, spatial, bodily/kinesthetic, interpersonal, and intrapersonal. In 1999, he added naturalistic and is informally considering two additional intelligences: existential and pedagogical. He has always cautioned that everyone has his or her own profile of intelligences and that an understanding of individual intelligences should be used to empower people, not to limit them. Understanding multiple intelligences theory allows teachers and administrators to believe in the importance of honoring each student as an individual and to consider the relatively narrow focus and limited value of standardized testing.

So why haven't these research-based game changers become common practice in our schools? Only now have we started to see mention of UDL in education as it is in the CCSS. Yet few teachers still understand what it means, and its discussion in the CCSS is not well articulated. There is a significant disconnect between research and policy and procedure and action. Education has traditionally been very slow to change. Rather, the pendulum swings back and forth from the basics to new programs in literacy and numeracy. We go from memorization of math facts to new math, from whole language to phonics, from emphasis on the arts to emphasis on science, from time for physical education to time for basics only. The pendulum moves faster these days, but the amplitude does not change.

We need a continuous improvement model based on new understandings and a constantly changing environment. We can change and be a bit more right in what we do. We can't think that we are wrong now and any change will make everything right. That's simply not the case. We must, however, keep up with the explosion of knowledge around us and even try to take the lead.

Through our experience as educators, researchers, and community members, we have developed a perspective that puts a premium on social justice, equity, and personal autonomy in the field of special education and the lives of people with what we call *disabilities*. Laws and policies attempt to provide social justice and equity, but legislation cannot guarantee or ensure these outcomes. As the saying goes, you cannot outlaw stupidity. On the other hand, it is our hope that we as professionals in the fields of education and human services can be effective advocates and champions of social justice and equity for all.

We question and challenge the semantics and the many underlying assumptions of the term *disability*. As a society, we have come a long way in leveling the playing field. In this sense, much of the ethos of special education has made a significant contribution to social justice. Ironically, many persons with learning differences do not qualify for special services. Unrecognized by the system, they often live in a world that dismisses much of who they are simply because they are different. We have made and are making progress in assuring the civil rights of persons with disabilities. We worry about many students and adults who do not qualify for special education support and who face discrimination because they learn differently but have little recourse to accommodations and adjustments. In some instances, personal wealth affords these children the type of support they need outside of school hours. We encourage you to question the use of the term *disabilities*. By the end of this book, we hope you will acquire a healthy amount of intellectual curiosity, challenge conventional wisdom and the status quo, and be ready to take on the work that still needs to be done.

2 Adult Developmental Theory and Learning Differences

I sometimes ask myself how it came about that I was the one to develop the theory of relativity. The reason, I think, is that a normal adult never stops to think about problems of space and time. These are things which he has thought about as a child.

—Albert Einstein

What is the relevance for exploring adult developmental theory as it relates to the educational and life experiences of individuals with learning differences? As teachers and parents, we are ultimately preparing children and adolescents with learning differences, to the greatest extent possible, for normal adult developmental experiences. Understandably, not every theory on adult development is the same, but the general similarities form a coherent sense about how we continue to develop throughout our lives. Consequently, we must assess curriculum and instruction in terms of preparing students for a lifespan of ongoing change that requires coping skills.

For many years, the conventional wisdom of developmental psychology asserted that the brain itself was fixed at an early age. An intelligence test from early childhood was thought to predict intelligence that was not expected to change over the lifespan. Cognitive skills and basic personality would stay the same in adulthood. Wisdom acquired with experience and age might help us use our intelligence more effectively, but our intelligence had not changed. The only real change we expected was the inexorable descent of abilities and skills in old age.

Current research indicates that the brain continues to transform throughout our twenties, forming new neural circuitries and pathways. Adolescence is a time of unparalleled creativity and explosive neural energy. Although there is less research on rewiring in later years, as the brain stores new knowledge and experiences, we reframe our thinking until it becomes qualitatively different than previously. Neuropsychological research is compelling us to rethink our developmental view of both young and later adulthood.

The relatively new field of adult development explores systematic psychological and sociological events that proceed predictably if not sequentially in adulthood. A variety of theories of adult development have informed the social sciences. Erik Erikson may be the best-known theorist in adult development. As with the field of child development, adult development abounds with diverse theories, many rooted in earlier child development theory but with an eye toward adulthood as a unique and discrete developmental period.

The broad areas of childhood, adolescence, early and middle adulthood, and late adulthood (what we now refer to as *aging* or *gerontology*) are distinct areas of lifespan development. Generally, we have less control in childhood and late adulthood. Extrinsic factors such as parents in childhood and declining health in late adulthood direct our lives.

Early and middle adulthood give us the greatest opportunities to exercise more intrinsically determined lives. It is at this time that we, as educators and mentors, must recognize the impact we can have on the lives of our students and children. The development of positive self-identity, confidence, and personal autonomy in childhood and especially in adolescence usually predicts the extent to which adults take advantage of these opportunities to assert a sense of control within their lives. Concurrently, our goals, accomplishments, and failures define much of our adult identity. In late adulthood, autonomous control often diminishes. Decisions begin to be made by others (often adult children) about residence, mobility, finances, and medical issues. The realities of increasing dependence may largely direct the latter part of life. The ability to adjust to this dependence can be positively impacted by the degree to which individuals have sculpted a successful relationship with themselves.

THEORIES OF ADULT DEVELOPMENT

Erik Erikson

Interest in adult development as a part of psychology and other social sciences has spurred many theories covering a range of diverse perspectives. Is life a continuous search for identity? Do we feel we know ourselves better as we age? Erik Erikson thought so. His theory of identity development begins in childhood and extends through adulthood. He described several stages pertinent to adulthood.

Erikson's three broad spans of adult identity correspond to the experiences of many, if not most people. Intimate relationships leading to (intended) long-term relationships and creating a family occur frequently

Erikson's Stages of Adult Development

Stage	Basic Conflict	Important Events	Outcome
Young Adulthood (19 to 40 years)	Intimacy versus Isolation	Relationships	Young adults need to form intimate, loving relationships with other people. Success leads to strong relationships, while failure results in loneliness and isolation.
Middle Adulthood (40 to 65 years)	Generativity versus Stagnation	Work and Parenthood	Adults need to create or nurture things that will outlast them, often by having children or creating a positive change that benefits other people. Success leads to feelings of usefulness and accomplishment, while failure results in shallow involvement in the world.
Maturity (65 years to death)	Ego Integrity versus Despair	Reflection on Life	Older adults need to look back on life and feel a sense of fulfillment. Success at this stage leads to feelings of wisdom, while failure results in regret, bitterness, and despair.

Adapted from Cherry, K. (2015). Erikson's psychosocial stages summary chart. *About.com.* Retrieved June 12, 2015, from http://psychology.about.com/od/psychosocialtheories/fl/Psychosocial-Stages-Summary-Chart.htm in our twenties to late thirties. The next or middle stage of caring for family, finding meaning in work or a career, and the beginning of taking a life inventory may guide us toward a sense of our lives ranging from satisfaction to mixed feelings to despair. We experience a great deal of ups and downs in this period. We can feel good about work, then not-so-good, and then good again. Erikson's views of the maturity stage are frighteningly stark: We die either feeling pretty good about ourselves or end our lives in utter despair—not the way we'd like to finish up. Life offers more nuances than Erikson's theory suggests. Most people die with their share of joy and sadness, satisfaction and regret, closure, and fear of the unknown. Nevertheless, we suspect the quality of life in the aging years deeply informs how we feel about ourselves in the latter stages of life.

Life may be a continuous search for identity, but Erikson's insistence on the importance of completing each stage before moving to the next conflicts with much personal experience, especially for adults with learning differences. If Erikson is taken literally, then many adults, with and without learning differences, would find themselves stuck in an earlier level of development, unable ever to move on and achieve a full sense of self. Clearly, our sense of self evolves without necessarily meeting all the conditions in each of these so-called stages.

However, a broader interpretation of Erikson may lead to a better understanding of why some adults with learning differences struggle so much. Some individuals never seem to achieve the expected maturity level of an adult. The reasons are endless. If children are overly protected and enabled by their parents (or even well-meaning teachers and advocates), they may become stuck in an earlier stage of development. It may be harder to move on within the Erikson model. Research has yet to explore the effects of modern parenting on adult outcomes of millennials and an even younger generation. Largely through anecdotes, many of us perceive today's young adults as less-than-prepared for getting on with adult life. When we perceive young adults as immature, we are seeing adulthood through a developmental lens.

Daniel Levinson

Daniel Levinson identified nine specific stages of adult development. "The life structure develops through a relatively orderly sequence of age-linked periods during the adult years" (Levinson, 1986, p. 7). Some stages are primarily coping with and settling into the structure of the particular stage. For example, in early adult years, we are not so much preparing for a later stage as much as trying to become grounded as an adult. However, once we attain several markers of early adulthood, such as finding steady employment and living independently, we get ready to transition to the next stage—building a family unit. Over time, we again settle into this structure, eventually getting ready for the next transition. We progress from one structure to another based on handling and making sense of structure-changing transitions. We transition to new structures or stages through self-appraisal and by considering possibilities for change. Levinson concluded that developmental transitions make up almost half of adulthood.

Levinson's theory has implications for children and adults with learning differences. Life is full of transitions. A major component of transition means taking risks, which leads to the same question we asked before: Are we overly protective of our children? Do we prevent them from taking risks? Are we denying them opportunities to learn to deal with the unexpected? Are we

Levinson's Theory of Adult Development

1. **Early adult transition (17–22)**: Creating a bridge between late adolescence and early adulthood

2. **Entering the adult world (22–28)**: Building and maintaining an adult world through initial choices in love, occupation, friendship, values, and lifestyle

3. **Age 30 transition (28–33)**: Reappraising previous life structure and plan for transition to settling down

4. **Culminating life structure for early adulthood (33–40)**: Focusing on marriage/family and career; appraising earlier goals; new roles contribute to maturity

5. **Midlife transition (40–45)**: Moving significantly from early adulthood to middle adulthood; more self-evaluation of overall quality of life, accomplishments, and overall satisfaction

6. **Entering middle adulthood (45–50)**: Achieving maturity

7. **The age 50 transition (50–55)**: Modifying and possibly improving entry life structure

8. **Culminating structure for middle adulthood (55–60)**: Concluding this stage and preparing for transition

9. **Late adult transition (60–65)**: Reflecting on past achievements and regrets and making peace with one's self and others (including God)

discouraging children from preparing for the many challenges and transitions found throughout adulthood?

What are some of the challenges and tests of adulthood? We all go through rites of passage, such as graduating from high school and perhaps higher education, getting our first job, finding a significant other (usually after a sequence of other relationships), establishing a career, having children, and parenting. The list goes on and on. In addition to these acknowledged components of adulthood are almost never-ending changes of less visibility but of no less importance. Careers change. Relationships change. Priorities change.

We are content at times for known and unknown reasons; we go through phases or periods of discontent that have no one cause. This duality certainly corresponds to the experiences of most of us. Theories differ on when and why we cycle from stability to transformation or from transformation to stability. We seem to need and seek both periods.

In his book, *Transitions: Making Sense of Life's Changes*, William Bridges presents a similar perspective. The book describes adult life as having three different psychological domains: Letting Go, The Neutral Zone, and Moving Forward (Bridges, 2004). Adulthood is all about change due to the events we encounter. Many crises are largely unavoidable but can occur at different points of the lifespan and with varying intensities. We can expect to experience some of them, but few experience all.

Overall, adulthood is a series of developmental tasks. These developmental tasks require adults to change preexisting ways of thinking and behaving to accommodate and manage the new demands of these tasks. Adult maturity corresponds to a stability in one stage that is rocked by a stage-specific crisis. We grow through how we handle each crisis and how flexible we are with our thinking and life plans.

Johnson and Blalock

Johnson and Blalock's (1987) groundbreaking investigations of adults with learning differences revealed two critical findings: (1) Learning disabilities did not end after school but persisted into adulthood and (2) adults with learning disabilities faced social, psychological, and vocational difficulties. One of the most common descriptors in the literature was, and continues to be, dysfunction.

The idea of persisting learning disabilities or differences was radical at this time. People believed that problems with learning affected children in school but disappeared after that. Somehow, kids outgrew their "disabilities." They did not look different. They did not seem to act differently. They blended into the adult world—or maybe they got lost.

IMPLICATIONS OF THEORIES OF ADULT DEVELOPMENT FOR INDIVIDUALS WITH LEARNING DIFFERENCES

Childhood social and psychological development, particularly in terms of interpersonal relationships and intrapersonal awareness and identity, forms the foundation for much of how we experience adulthood. Education—past, present, and future—serves as a catalyst for much of the adult experience. Environmental factors include but not are not limited to family dynamics, experiential learning, and community.

Having a child with learning differences naturally brings out the tendency to be protective. This is a child who is vulnerable. This is a child who is struggling. Parents want to bear at least some of that weight and become fighters and champions for their child. We need, however, to be careful not to shield children from the realities of learning differently or of being different. Effective parenting may be a willingness to step back and let children take risks ranging from trying to make a new friend to taking on challenges in the classroom. We need to comfort them when they fail, but we need to let them fail and try again. Effective teaching means teaching students multiple ways to solve problems and dilemmas and to evaluate choices. This leads to a sense of self-control and resilience—key factors for successful adult outcomes (Reiff, Gerber, & Ginsberg, 1997; Spekman, Goldberg, & Herman, 1993).

Many factors drive our sense of who we are as adults. The adult world consists of intersecting domains. The area that almost anyone would identify as a large—if not the largest area—is the world of work, employment, vocation, or career. In addition, the multitude and types of relationships that we find, maintain, and often lose have a tremendous impact not only on how we see ourselves but on many of the choices we make about our place in the adult world. We also know that all work and no play denies so much of what life has to offer, albeit in a developmental series of challenges. Recreation not only seems to be a critical piece of balanced functioning, it also helps, in many cases, to round out a sense of personal identity. Physical well-being clearly has developmental overtones and plays another important factor affecting overall quality of life. Certainly not all-inclusive, such a list could be expanded depending on theoretical, philosophical, and religious orientation. Let's examine adult development of persons with learning differences within some of these domains.

Work and Career

Adults with learning differences contend with the same kinds of challenges in the world of work as those without learning differences. But some of these challenges are likely to have additional obstacles, such as time management, organization and planning, and following directions. These characteristics can lead to poor work performance and loss of employment. It is difficult to rebound from a job loss if skills are limited, especially in a down economy. As a result of the realities of employment demands, many adults with learning differences have additional anxiety and stress connected with simply being who they are. Individuals with learning differences can have intense difficulty with executive functions but outstanding strengths in personality, creativity, problem-solving skills, and drive. When nurtured across the lifespan, these strengths can lead to meaningful and successful employment. Poor executive functioning, however, can lead to difficulties at work and home, often creating an insidious cycle in which stress leads to negative outcomes, which lead to more stress.

These realities of coping with the ever-changing demands of work and career have clear implications for teaching and the transition process. Perhaps the most important understanding our children need to develop is that adult life is anything but a placid, straightforward journey. Erikson, Levinson, and Bridges recognized that ups and downs were the norm. When adults with learning differences take an inventory of their lives, what preparation will help them to look back in satisfaction rather than despair? How can we cultivate and acknowledge the variety of individual strengths that occur alongside challenging learning differences?

First, it is important to foster individual strengths intentionally as part of the school day. Second, these strengths need to be articulated as we transition students through middle and high school with the awareness that satisfaction need not be linked to a single career. In the new normal, adults may find more satisfaction in their abilities to adapt to moving from one job to another. Transition planning means building a multitude of workplace skills and acknowledging one's strengths and needs but not necessarily a specific expertise. Instead, adroitness at applying general abilities to a variety of settings will be more helpful. Although today's job market increasingly relies on technology skills, those skills are constantly changing. Many employers are less impressed by a specific skill set and more interested in problem solving and effective decision making. Clearly, instruction delivered to students with learning differences should emphasize problem solving and effective decision making.

As teachers and parents, we need to make sure students have opportunities to build technological skills, but we also have a responsibility to direct them to develop effective skills for the workplace. Many careers want individuals who know how to use various types of word processing, spreadsheets, and software. They need to know how to find information beyond the first site presented by Google. They must discriminate relevant from irrelevant information and assess credibility, validity, and applications of websites. While some students are able to pick up these skills through incidental learning, students with learning differences often have difficulties with these kinds of processing and evaluation skills.

The world of work and career has changed dramatically in the last forty years. Many developmental theories were predicated on having one career for a lifetime, often the same job. However, a gold watch for fifty years of employment with one company has become unusual. In a 2015 report from the Bureau of Labor Statistics of the U.S. Department of Labor, "individuals born from 1957 to 1964 held an average of 11.7 jobs from ages 18 to 48. These baby boomers held an average of 5.5 jobs while ages 18 to 24" (2015a). (In this report, a *job* is defined as an uninterrupted period of work with a particular employer.) Jobs are not the same as careers and may change within the same organization. Businesses have restructured to hire fewer people than previously. As much as unemployment figures have dropped in recent years, underemployment continues to be pervasive. Multiple job changes are more the norm than the exception.

Research and experience tell us that many children with learning differences have particular difficulties with being flexible and adapting to change. It often takes longer to acquire skills that work; as a result, it may be harder to let go and move on. Problems with nonverbal language and social interaction contribute to a degree of rigidity. Nonverbal language difficulties include

---

Advice From Temple Grandin: Learning to Be Flexible

How can common sense be taught? I think it starts with teaching flexibility at a young age. Structure is good for children with autism, but sometimes plans can and need to be changed. When I was little, my nanny made my sister and me do a variety of activities. This variety prevented rigid behavior patterns from forming. I became more accustomed to changes in our daily or weekly routines and learned that I could still manage when change occurred.

Another way to teach flexibility of thinking is to use visual metaphors, such as mixing paint. To understand complex situations, such as when occasionally a good friend does something nasty, I imagine mixing white and black paint. If the friend's behavior is mostly nice, the mixture is a very light gray; if the person is really not a friend, then the mixture is a very dark gray.

Flexibility can also be taught by showing the person with autism that categories can change. Objects can be sorted by color, function, or material. To test this idea, I grabbed a bunch of black, red, and yellow objects in my office and laid them on the floor. They were a stapler, a roll of tape, a ball, videotapes, a toolbox, a hat, and pens. Depending upon the situation, any of these objects could be used for either work or play. Ask the child to give concrete examples of using a stapler for work or play. For instance, stapling office papers is work; stapling a kite together is play. Simple situations like this that teach a child flexibility in thinking and relating can be found numerous times in each day.

There are times when an absolute adherence to the rule can cause harm. Children also need to be taught that some rules can change depending on the situation. Emergencies are one such category where rules may be allowed to be broken. Parents, teachers, and therapists can continually teach and reinforce flexible thinking patterns in children with autism/AS.

Excerpted from Grandin, T. (2002). Advice from Temple Grandin: Learning to be flexible. *Autism Asperger's Digest*, July–August. Retrieved June 12, 2015, from http://www.autismtoday.com/library-back/Teaching_Flexibility.htm

difficulty understanding facial expressions, body language, and tone of voice. Most of us can roll with the ever-shifting nuances of nonverbal communication and interaction. On other hand, individuals with difficulties in nonverbal communication and interaction may not even process the ever-changing dynamics of their environment. If they are able to change their approach, they may go in a wrong direction. Any difference in a daily routine can cause havoc for many persons on the autism spectrum. Temple Grandin, the eminent animal scientist, professor, best-selling author, and autistic activist, has direct approaches to teaching flexibility to people with Asperger's syndrome.

Learning differences do not always have an impact on career choices. Vocations requiring minimal reading abilities do not limit adults with reading difficulties. Nevertheless, the nature of many jobs is changing and demanding more reading skills. For example, auto mechanics may spend the majority of their time under the hood, but they also need to read computer diagnostics, communicate online when ordering parts, and stay abreast of industry standards. Additionally, technical training in both high school and postsecondary programs relies on students' ability to read manuals and reports. As a result, the choice of traditional careers may be shrinking for some adults with learning differences. Some adults with learning differences feel trapped. The world does not acknowledge their gifts but focuses on their weaknesses, which happen to reflect the qualities that society deems important—particularly language and math skills.

Unemployment and underemployment, in spite of the era of Section 504 of the Rehabilitation Act of 1973 and the Americans with Disabilities Act (ADA) of 1990, remain pervasive. The phenomenon of underemployment is particularly pernicious, as being stuck in a world of part-time, underpaid, under-skilled, and tedious dead-end work can be equally if not more exasperating than simply not working at all. We might expect more positive outcomes in the era of ADA, but statistics belie that belief.

The Bureau of Labor Statistics of the U.S. Department of Labor (2015b) reported these findings from 2014:

- The employment-population ratio for persons with a disability was less than half that of those with no disability.
- Thirty-four percent of workers with a disability were employed part time, compared with 19% of those with no disability.
- Employed persons with a disability were more likely to be self-employed than those with no disability.

Employment outcomes of persons with learning differences continue to be discouraging. The difference between a high school and college diploma plays a significant factor, as it does with all persons in the workforce. That is, adults with learning differences who have a postsecondary degree fare better in the workplace than those with only a high school education. However, individuals with learning differences are less likely to attend college. They may be placed at a double disadvantage. A more ominous outcome arises from observations of the prison population. Hard data are not readily available, but estimates suggest that from 50% to 80% of prisoners in the U.S. have some sort of learning difference, generally undiagnosed.

Study after study found that young adults with learning differences did not attend college or postsecondary education as often as their peers. After high school, individuals with learning differences were often unemployed or underemployed. The majority lived at home with parents (Hoy et al., 1997). Over time, they made significantly less money. Social, civic, and interpersonal interactions were limited and restricted. A lack of life adjustment skills such as problem-solving techniques, weak cognitive processes, and a lack of systematic problem-solving continued to have negative implications in any number of adult domains (Roffman, Herzog, & Wershba-Gershon, 1994). Adults with learning differences who lack goals and vocational aptitude may live from crisis to crisis.

Education

The educational experiences of persons with learning differences inform all of adulthood. Education is at best a challenge, more often a struggle. It is in this arena that difficulties generally come to light. Abilities with language in all its forms, math and science, and learning strategies are constantly assessed. More than fifty years of research has documented these difficulties for students.

What happens in school on the road to adulthood? What is the intersection of the developmental process and the demands of school? Where does the development of the self come together or fall apart? In order for teachers to foster successful adult development, these school benchmarks need to be recognized.

Early education emphasizes the development of basic and functional academic skills. These skills provide the foundation for higher levels of learning: problem solving, decision making, comprehension, distinguishing the relevant from the irrelevant, and so on. Utilization of these skills becomes increasingly important as the student progresses through the education system, including postsecondary and graduate levels.

Students with learning differences who fall behind the curve in building basic reading skills become doubly at risk as they progress. Reading continues to be difficult, slow, and often exhausting. Naturally, many students find reading aversive and have trouble maintaining concentration and completing projects and assignments. The problems multiply when they are expected to learn independently through reading. Lack of comprehension limits the higher-order skills just discussed. Early intervention for children who are at-risk is a common consensus. In fact, it is so pervasive that we cannot add a great deal to the discussion, other than to agree. The paradox when dealing with hidden disabilities is the risk of jumping in prematurely. Diagnostic testing does not always reveal a reliable and valid picture of a young child's learning style. Oftentimes, it addresses weaknesses without adequately portraying what a child is good at or how a teacher may cultivate the positive qualities of a child to foster success as a young adult.

Identity Issues: Interpersonal Relationships

In addition to a focus on work and career, virtually all theories of adult development emphasize the importance of significant relationships. An obvious shortcoming of most models is the assumption that the traditional nuclear family constitutes the norm. We know that this conception is losing relevance for increasing numbers of adults, particularly younger adults. Divorce affects approximately 50% of American couples. Few spouses go through a divorce unscathed. Problems with social skills and interpersonal relationships—traits sometimes associated with learning differences—have clear implications for making this period even more challenging. Eventually, they may get their life back on track, in many cases by creating a new family unit. Some individuals do not create new relationships.

We live increasingly in an age of single parents, partners who are not married, and dramatic shifts in family stability. Not only does this impact individuals with learning differences as a result of the typical stresses associated with being a single parent, but it also places increased demands on executive functions and functional reading and math skills. Often, divorce not only represents the loss of relationship but also the loss of assistance with household tasks such as budgeting, reading insurance plans, submitting medical claims, and paying bills on time. Significant relationships are generally critical to a satisfying and meaningful sense of adulthood. The developmental nature of adult relationships presents greater complexity than childhood relationships.

Deficits with social relationships can have a devastating impact on personal life. Being connected is fundamental to a meaningful adult existence. Learning and preparing ways to build interdependent relationships need to be intentional for many persons with learning differences. The not-uncommon trait of difficulties with nonverbal language and social fluency tends to sour interpersonal connections. We have met with too many students with learning differences who are distressed by their inability to form deep friendships and intimate relationships. On the other hand, motivated adults with learning differences have learned effective social skills, but consciously and intentionally learning and using these skills represent a qualitatively different adult experience.

For potential partners, the difficulty with maintaining intimate relationships with a person who has difficulties with nonverbal language and social fluency can be challenging or unappealing. Problems relating to another person can undermine feelings of fulfillment. This influences how adults with certain types of learning differences view themselves and their transition to the next developmental stage. Family life is frequently different when one or both parents have learning differences. The relationship between parent and child may be more difficult to develop in some cases.

Learning differences in children are often associated with poor social skills and low self-concept. Many of the same negative outcomes of childhood continue to impact adulthood. In studies (including those by Johnson and Blalock), adults with learning differences reported feeling more rejected and less accepted, a clear link to their dissatisfaction with social and interpersonal aspects of their lives. They talked about pervasive feelings of loneliness, social alienation, and isolation. They were not happy with their jobs or careers. Perhaps most troubling was their sense that they did not know why their lives were so unsatisfying, even sad.

In his new book, *The Journal of Best Practices*, David Finch (2012), an adult with Asperger's, made an intentional and conscious effort to overcome quirky social behaviors. As with many "Aspies," he lacks empathy and can be quite oblivious to others' feelings, intentions, and preferences. He taught himself to be more responsive to his wife's needs. He literally created scripts that fit situations more appropriately than his natural inclinations. When his wife came home from work, he learned that to ask, "How was your day?" Her predictable reply was, "It was a pain." Instead of going off on one of his own quirky topics, he learned that all she wanted was for him to sound empathetic: "Gee, that sounds tough." He memorized a comment that conveys empathy, even though he did not really connect with the emotion. When an interviewer asked his wife if it felt disingenuous for her husband to script displays of empathy, she responded that caring enough to want to make her feel better was a profound act of love.

We do not know of any quick remedies for learning how to attend to and understand these cues. But they can be learned. The first step is simply to recognize whether there are difficulties with nonverbal language. Parents and teachers can provide honest feedback. Learning differences in adulthood require a greater need for self-reflection. Fortunately, there are programs that can help adolescents and adults improve their nonverbal social decoding skills. For example, *Mind Reading* (Cohen, 2007) has three different training components: an emotions library to look at specific emotions, a learning center with lessons and quizzes, and games to help identify emotions. FACELAND, a game-like computer program by Do2Learn, focuses on recognizing and understanding surprise, anger, fear, disgust, sadness, and happiness. Individuals look at photos with an emotion and identify the emotion that is shown in the photo. FACELAND may help lower anxiety and improve facial recognition.

Learning differences have a significant impact on self-concept, self-esteem, and a sense of personal autonomy throughout life. We are all the product of the sum total of our life experiences. When so many of those experiences are colored by learning differences, the internal psychological product takes on those hues. Feelings of inferiority from childhood inform self-concept and self-image throughout adult development. In some cases, they are reinforced. In others, they are reframed. Regardless, they affect relationships for the lifespan.

Identity Issues: Self-Perception and Disclosure

Erikson viewed adulthood explicitly as a continuing search for identity. Although not as prominent in other theories, the continuous formation of identity is almost always implicit. Most persons would agree that their identity is not fixed in their early twenties. As much as we may expect to have a permanent identity formation by early middle age, our sense of self continues to evolve.

Childhood experiences have a significant impact on how we will see ourselves as adults. Variables connected to child development (such as level of self-confidence, degree of autonomy, and overall outlook) determine the extent to which we are ready to begin adulthood on a positive or negative track. One of the only commonalities of the world of learning differences is a different type of childhood. Too often, many early experiences are negative and long lasting. Children with learning differences are often treated as outsiders and marginalized. For some, this actually strengthens resolve and positive identity formation. For others, not so much. As researchers, we have been very interested in why some folks succeed while others fail when they appear to come from the same circumstances.

In school, the impact of learning differences is generally clear. In addition, children with a specific diagnosis bear a label, which is part of their sense of identity for better or worse. The effects of learning differences are not as obvious later in life. The label becomes invisible unless the adult chooses to share it. An adult may believe that learning differences do not have an impact on his or her life currently. An adult may choose to reject the label that dictated many childhood experiences. If the impact is acknowledged, to what extent are one's learning differences disclosed? When? Where? To whom?

Think about the far-reaching consequences of this decision. It has the potential to affect virtually every domain of adult life. In college, it may mean the difference between accessing support and trying to make it alone. Academic and social support services in higher education have a positive impact. In order to receive services, in most cases, the student has to self-identify as having a recent psychoeducational evaluation documenting learning differences. It should not be surprising that any number of students do not want to broadcast what may have been a stigmatizing label or diagnosis. Stigma associated with feeling "less than one's peers" or "trying to get an unfair advantage over others because of a learning difference" often prevents individuals from requesting genuinely needed accommodations, even in a college setting. Luckily, as learning differences become a more common part of our vocabulary, understanding, and familiarity, more and more college students do self-disclose, with pressure often coming from parents to seek support.

Entering the workforce, the decision to disclose becomes an issue again. Fewer individuals with learning differences do this, fearing (often rightly) that disclosure will hurt their application chances as well as draw unwanted attention from peers, supervisors, or supervisees. In addition, determining and providing workplace accommodations and adjustments is generally elusive for all involved.

Learning differences probably will affect work if not disclosed or if dismissed by the individual as being unimportant. For example, we all know fellow employees who exhibit symptoms of attention deficit/hyperactivity disorder (ADHD). They may or may not have a diagnosis. They may or may not talk about it. But it will have an impact on time management, general organization, and, most of all, anxiety and self-esteem. Dr. Garry J. McClean, a health and safety consultant and writer for *The Workplace Depot* and various magazines, writes about workplace issues for adults with ADHD (2015). He points out that increased irritability, isolation and withdrawal, frequent sickness, and a general perception that the workplace is a hostile environment are the types of reactions that may be related to learning differences. Workplace stress is certainly not unique to adults with learning differences, but it may be qualitatively different and more dysfunctional.

Many adults struggle with the disclosure issue in interpersonal situations because they fear rejection and being defined solely by their learning differences. Disclosure will color any relationship, but not disclosing can lead to significant miscommunication and misunderstanding. Well-adapted individuals with learning differences have learned to overcome that fear.

Quinn Bradlee, the founder of a website for young adults with learning differences, *Friends of Quinn*, shares his personal view of self-disclosing:

How do you open up and talk about your [learning differences] with someone for the first time?

When I was in high school I went on a three week "nautical school" trip to Tahiti. I was going to be around a group of people I didn't know for a while, so the first thing that I did before we set sail was tell them that I have dyslexia.

I told them because I didn't want them to think that I was weird, and if I did anything that seemed off, they would have a better understanding of why. I told them that I had trouble with reading and social cues. I also told them that the more I talked about my dyslexia I would hopefully inspire other people to talk about their [learning differences]. Years later, it's my sense that there are more and more people who know what dyslexia and other learning disabilities are, and people who have [learning differences] are more comfortable talking about it.

When and why would you need to tell somebody about your [learning differences]? One of the hardest parts of having a [learning difference] is knowing when to tell someone, especially someone that you are dating. I try to get it out of the way early, when I'm first getting to know someone. We'll get in to the usual intro questions, like where are you from, where did you go to school? That's a good opening, because you can talk about whether you were in a [learning differences] program or a special school. Or you can talk about your experiences in school and how you learn differently.

The other tricky situation when you may want to tell someone about your [learning differences] is at your job. I remember that it was not that long ago I was working in an office, and for me it was easy to tell them that I had a [learning difference] because that's why I was there in the first place. My parents knew the person that I was going to work for, so we went and had a few meetings to get to know him better and so that he could understand me. During the meetings we talked about what I would be doing and we also talked about my skills; what I am good at and what I'm not good at.

I think sometimes you just need to come out and talk about your [learning differences]. Just say: "I need to be honest with you and let you know that I have a learning difference." For example, maybe your boss hands out a report at a meeting that everyone is supposed to read. Maybe you would tell your boss that you have dyslexia and have trouble reading, but if he or she sends you the report electronically, you could have your computer read it out loud to you. (I do this all the time!) That way you show them that you can still do your job, you just process information differently and need work-arounds sometimes.

Anyone who knows me knows that I'm different in a lot of ways from most people. This may not work for most people, but when I feel the need to tell someone about my [learning differences], I just go right ahead and tell them straight up. I don't feel ashamed that I learn differently. My [learning differences] give me challenges, but they are also a gift! (Bradlee, 2013)

THE LATE AGING PROCESS

Perhaps the least-discussed facet of the intersection of adult development and learning differences is the late aging process. In the past few decades, not only has life expectancy increased but the expectations of what life can be for older persons have changed. We now see developmental changes in old age, but instead of inevitable deterioration, possibilities for new growth and stimulation are becoming an increasing part of the landscape of geriatrics. Aging baby-boomers increasingly reject the notion of growing old, at least the way their parents did. We have much less information on the late-life experiences of persons with learning differences. We do know that adults with Down's syndrome face qualitatively different risks than do the general population. Nonetheless, evidence is growing that risk, onset, and type of dementia is subtly different for many people with learning differences. It may be more difficult to diagnose idiosyncratic behaviors of early dementia if the individual already exhibits idiosyncratic behaviors. Preexisting problems in areas such as executive functioning, nonverbal and verbal language, and reasoning are likely to exacerbate dementia. Even in the final stages of life, the intersection of learning differences and adult development continues to create qualitatively different experiences.

3 Keys to Success

Challenges are what make life interesting and overcoming them is what makes life meaningful.

—Joshua J. Marine

Success in adulthood takes on many forms and dimensions. This chapter examines different perspectives of success by highlighting the widely acknowledged theories and philosophies of Abraham Maslow, Steven Covey, Dale Carnegie, and Deepak Chopra and analyzes their relevance to students and adults with learning differences. Success takes many forms, both externally (work, wealth, accomplishments) as well as internally (self-contentment, overall satisfaction, a positive sense of place in the world). In spite of this breadth of constructs, perspectives converge around several basic themes. Individuals with learning differences have the potential and opportunities to learn and utilize components of these models.

ABRAHAM MASLOW

Abraham Maslow (1954) is known for his theory about a hierarchy of needs. His work has risen to the level of being conventional wisdom, albeit not without some controversy. Nonetheless, Maslow's conceptualization of how humans are motivated to become successful dovetails with general psychological thought and common sense. He studied successful individuals who tended to be highly motivated and self-actualized.

According to Maslow's hierarchy of needs model, individuals will have great difficulty until their basic needs are met. Homeless and destitute individuals have difficulty finding the energy or rationale to plan long-term goals for success. They have little choice but to focus on finding the next meal and shelter for the night. Marginalized citizens feel a sense of shame or failure, hardly a foundation for healthy self-esteem and a sense of empowerment. Too often, children who struggle in school come from disadvantaged backgrounds. Most schools recognize that empty stomachs preclude learning.

Readers of this book are probably not in such unfortunate circumstances. However, the next level of Maslow's hierarchy speaks to building success in our children and students. Belongingness and love make up the next building block. Many children with learning differences question the degree to which they belong and are accepted. Negative reactions to their differences may undermine their capacity to accept themselves for who they are. An inability to move beyond this stage prevents moving to a sense of self-esteem, the basis and desire to achieve and succeed.

The implications are clear for parents and teachers. It is all too easy to communicate messages of doubt unintentionally. We wish that our children could do better. We wonder why they struggle, especially prior to a diagnosis. How many times do students with learning differences report that their teachers tell them that they are lazy, stupid, or incompetent? The first step for parents and teachers is to be aware of the messages children and students with learning differences may hear. Without intentional intervention, children will internalize this negative perception. Later in this book, we will discuss building relationships and unconditional love.

As we move through the hierarchy, we depend on cognitive knowledge about ourselves and how we fit into the world. Students with learning differences deserve to learn about their strengths and weaknesses. Paradoxically, they are usually out of the loop. They often do not attend their Individual Education Program (IEP) conferences, where decisions are made for them, not with them. Not only does this phenomenon continue to create doubt about self-efficacy and control over their own lives, it denies them the information they need to develop strategies and coping skills connected to their individual and unique learning styles and needs. Involvement in the evaluation and IEP process benefits children by helping them with their need to discover themselves and their fit in the world. Children and adults with learning differences will function optimally when they have the freedom to show what they can do best in a variety of ways. A holistic and encouraging learning environment fosters traits that are associated with life success. With these skills in place, our students will build self-actualization and greater confidence of how to take on the world as adults.

STEVEN COVEY

The Seven Habits of Highly Effective People (Covey, 1989) has had an enormous impact for very clear reasons. It makes a compelling case that a discrete number of learned skills make a dramatic difference in desired outcomes. The fluency and ease of acquiring these attributes may present greater challenges when learning differences enter the picture. Nonetheless, *The Seven Habits* has much to offer children and adults with learning differences. The model presents a set of attributes to become an effective and successful person.

The Seven Habits of Highly Effective People

Habit 1: Be Proactive

Proactive people

- take responsibility for their life,
- focus their time and energy on things they can control, and
- are aware of the areas in which they expend their energies.

Habit 2: Begin With the End in Mind

People who begin with the end in mind

- envision in their mind what they cannot at present see,
- connect with their own uniqueness, and
- plan for success.

Habit 3: Put First Things First

People who put first things first

- organize and manage time and events according to the personal priorities established in Habit 2,
- focus on their highest priorities, and
- realize that it's all right to say no.

Habit 4: Think Win-Win

People who think win-win

- see life as a cooperative arena, not a competitive one;
- express ideas and feelings with courage and consideration for the ideas and feelings of others; and
- seek mutual benefit in all human interactions.

(Continued)

(Continued)

Habit 5: Seek First to Understand and Then to Be Understood

People who seek first to understand and then to be understood

- listen with the intent to understand, not to reply;
- do not decide prematurely what the other person means; and
- acknowledge and embrace other frames of reference.

Habit 6: Synergize

People who synergize

- cooperate creatively and effectively with others;
- initiate and encourage teamwork, open-mindedness, and new solutions; and
- value differences.

Habit 7: Sharpen the Saw

People who sharpen the saw

- renew themselves physically, socially/emotionally, mentally, and spiritually;
- create growth and change in their lives; and
- have the desire, knowledge, and skill to balance their lives and take care of themselves.

Covey's first habit, *Be Proactive*, is all about accountability. Rather than have others make decisions for us, we need to make choices. We are responsible for the choices we make, including those that result in failure. The willingness to take responsibility increases a sense of control. Students with learning differences are prone to doing the opposite, commonly known as *learned helplessness*. In a firm but loving way, teachers and parents need to reinforce personal responsibility in students with learning differences. It is too easy to use the difficulties presented by learning differences as a crutch. The effects of learned helplessness may last a lifetime, fostering dependence, feelings of inadequacy, and a less-than-attractive persona. The assumption of personal responsibility may also last a lifetime, with far better outcomes.

The second and third habits of *Begin With the End in Mind* and *Put First Things First* speak to the importance of setting ambitious but realistic goals and developing strategies to accomplish them. We have met with many students with learning differences who have ambitious goals but no plans or strategies to achieve them. They do not connect their goals to their unique strengths and skill sets. Both elementary and secondary schooling provide many opportunities to become more astute and focused on goals. Time management, organization, and prioritizing reinforce the power of planning for long-term rather than immediate goals. Making the connection of strengths and weaknesses with goal choices and the strategies to achieve them has added significance for students with learning differences. They may not have the luxury of wandering from interest to interest without encountering undue frustration in areas of weakness.

Students with learning differences need to be aware of the greater effort required to achieve goals. More than their peers, they must learn to say no and avoid overextending themselves. Demanding students to be involved in every activity possible—three seasons of sports, countless extracurriculars, internships, and part-time work—has become rampant in our culture. The infamous helicopter parent starts setting up expectations early in the child's life to prepare to be accepted into the best colleges.

The novel, *Admission*, by Jean Korelitz (2009) is based on her real-life experiences as a part-time reader in the Office of Admissions at Princeton University, an institution that admits less than one tenth of all applicants. Virtually all applicants are told from the outset that they must do everything they can to get into a school such as Princeton. Nine out of ten of these highly successful and extraordinary students will fail in their quest. Portia, the semiautobiographical admissions counselor in the book, voices her concern:

> And I don't think there is anyone in my field right now who isn't worried about what this is doing to the kids. And I don't just mean the competition, though that's bad enough. I mean what the process is doing to them psychologically . . . the *message*. To the kids: . . . They've been tutored in everything, for years, whether they need it or not. So what they come to understand is: I'm not good enough to do it on my own. I need help to be successful. . . . And how can that not carry forward into their adult lives? . . . They don't feel smart or capable in the least. (p. 308)

The clear implication: Expect your child to succeed, but do not put all your eggs in the basket of what you consider success. Parenting and teaching students with learning differences is a delicate balancing act between pushing too hard or not enough. As with any child, they need direction and modeling from adults. As with any child, they need to figure out their own paths in life. Allow them to be creative and autonomous in their ambitions. Do not ask them to be different than who they are.

We are not advocating a laissez-faire approach, particularly in regard to preparing for college. Tests such as the SAT and ACT remain a critical component of college admissions. Students with learning differences are notoriously flummoxed by standardized tests. They may improve their results by learning how to take tests. Commercial agencies such as Kaplan and the Princeton Review advertise "guaranteed" gains. Some companies claim average increases of about 200 points on the SAT, although critics question the accuracy of the data. Regardless, review courses or private tutoring are helpful for many students, especially those who lack sophisticated test-taking skills. A few guides are geared directly to students with learning differences, such as *Barron's SAT Strategies for Students With Learning Disabilities* (Welkes, 2008) and *LD SAT Study Guide* (Osborne, 2009). They have received limited but positive reviews.

Covey's next step, *Think Win-Win*, relies on highly refined social skills. Students with learning differences too often come from a lose-lose perspective. They draw inward and become dependent. Parents and teachers need to help them lessen dependence. The goal is interdependence rather than independence.

In order to attain a sense of interdependence and autonomy, young adults with learning differences must go through their own journey to self-acceptance and self-actualization. Making it in life boils down to being an effective self-advocate. The process starts with acknowledging childhood hurt, pain, and even grief. It continues with moving on and learning about personal strengths and weaknesses. Students with learning differences need to know what works and what doesn't, when to ask for help, how to ask for help, how to help others, when to back off, when to persist, and when to stand alone. This is interdependence. No one wants to live entirely alone nor completely enabled by others. Instead, we need to build a sense of cooperation by teaching cooperative skills. Cooperative activities require participation, where a sense of interdependence arises. Students with learning differences observe and begin to internalize that they have as much to offer as anyone else.

Habit Five, *Seek First to Understand and Then to Be Understood*, also requires social skills. This habit addresses the ability to listen and refrain from responding from our preconceived perceptions. This habit is ultimately about connecting and being open to other perspectives and requires several abilities: to process what another is communicating, to resist interjecting and being judgmental, and to respond in way that values the other person. We are all guilty of speaking or interjecting from our own frame of reference. We are all guilty of responding without truly having listened. Students who do not control impulsivity are notorious for butting in, sometimes in irrelevant ways, for various processing reasons. Nothing kills social or professional interactions more than demonstrating a seeming disregard for the other person. We will explore techniques for inhibiting impulses when we discuss executive functioning.

Habit Six, *Synergize,* reminds us that we achieve more by working together than alone. As Covey points out, the whole is greater than the sum of its parts. Similar to *Think Win-Win,* cooperative ventures work best when each individual's contribution is valued. We speak of the need to value the strengths of persons with learning differences. The converse holds true: We need to teach students with learning differences to value the strengths of others.

Many persons with learning differences match up well with the concept of synergy. They are creative and divergent thinkers and should be encouraged to tap into these attributes. Typical thinkers tend to be more convergent, wanting to settle on a single best approach. Coming up with multiple potential solutions to a given problem has increased relevance, especially in the nonlinear world of technology. Cooperative groups in school require teacher direction: assigning roles, gatekeeping, facilitating processes, and defining reporting of conclusions. Teachers are in a wonderful position to offer opportunities for their students to learn to synergize.

Finally, Habit 7, *Sharpen the Saw,* speaks to renewal and re-creation (the root of the more common term). Parents, especially, need to model a balance in life. Children learn healthy eating, physical activity, lifelong learning, curiosity, and inquisitiveness from their parents and, to a lesser extent, from their teachers. With encouragement, children will internalize and habitualize these traits into adulthood. So many adults love to camp or follow a hobby or take an interest in sports because they have positive family memories and they want to pass these memories on to their children. "Wish I had spent more time at the office" rarely appears on headstones.

DALE CARNEGIE

Dale Carnegie wrote a book in 1936 that continues to be popular and relevant and has significant credibility today. It predates many of Covey's strategies. The tenets of *How to Win Friends and Influence People* are simple. Criticizing others does not achieve goals; appreciating others honestly and sincerely does. Carnegie recognized the importance of recognizing another's perspective.

Carnegie was equally interested in the importance of making friends. This perspective holds special relevance for children and adults with learning differences, who, as we have seen, often feel isolated and lack friends. Showing a sincere appreciation for others underlies the skill of making friends. Carnegie's basic tenet is making other people feel important. Empathy plays a large role; this quality is elusive for a number of folks with learning differences, particularly Asperger's syndrome and other autism spectrum disorders.

Teaching a person who is not tuned in to the social nuances of empathy is challenging at best. However, it is possible to learn social graces such as greeting people with enthusiasm. It is possible to learn to be more outgoing. We can learn to smile, a trait on which Carnegie places great importance.

Winning friends and influencing people does not come easily. People with nonverbal social skills difficulties are notorious for interpreting spoken language too concretely. "Just jump into the conversation," could result in a student literally jumping in between two people—not exactly a recipe for social acceptance. Being overly enthusiastic and outgoing makes others uncomfortable. How will students learn the differences between being engaging and overbearing? Modeling prosocial behaviors intentionally and with explanation is a wise path for teachers and parents to follow. The more they expose their children (and even adults) to positive ways to interact, the greater the likelihood that individuals will internalize some of those behaviors. And the more people with learning differences find success, the more they will be reinforced. Reinforcement leads to maintaining and improving behaviors. Carnegie knew that making friends does not always come naturally. That's why he provided instructions.

Successful people need to have the capacity to get *buy-in* from others (Carnegie's concept of "winning people to your way of thinking"). We probably know something about all his recommendations, but we need to be reminded: Avoid arguments. Find common ground. Show respect. Understand other points of view. Work cooperatively to develop shared ideas. *How to Make Friends and Influence People* offers additional advice, consistently with the message not much removed from the Golden Rule: "Treat others as you would want to be treated." Most of us deviate occasionally (or often) from this code, even though we know better. If we expect our children and students to learn these positive behaviors, we need to make a *disciplined* effort to model and provide every opportunity for students to use them.

DEEPAK CHOPRA

The broader concept of adulthood in terms of overall satisfaction, contentment, happiness, and spiritual centeredness is also a model of achieving success. We are examining more than the standard notions of success and exploring a much broader concept of adulthood. Adults with learning differences and the alternative medicine guru Deepak Chopra do not typically wind up in the same sentence. However, his notions of positive outcomes bear more than a passing relevance. These outcomes do not receive a great deal of attention in most studies. This disparity is counterintuitive. We know with some certainty that wealth in and of itself does not make people happy. Further, although successful people generally find much satisfaction in their work, it may not carry over into other domains.

Chopra has written about achieving material success but with the caveat that success is more than material acquisition. "Success also includes good health, energy and enthusiasm for life, fulfilling relationships, creative freedom, emotional and psychological stability, a sense of well-being, and peace of mind" (Chopra, 1994, p. 2). In this sense, he taps into many adult development theories. In *The Seven Laws of Spiritual Success*, Chopra offers his vision for the basis of a good life both internally and externally.

Chopra's laws have the potential to pave a smoother path through life for adults with learning differences. Teachers and parents can use Chopra's

---

The Seven Laws of Spiritual Success

Law 1. Pure Potentiality

People who strive for pure potentiality

- are in touch with their true self,
- realize that they cannot control external events, and
- place little value in external manifestations of success.

Law 2. Giving

People who are giving

- understand that all successful relationships are based on give and take,
- find joy in giving sincerely, and
- create ways to give to others in all interactions.

Law 3. Karma or Cause and Effect

People who tune into karma or cause and effect

- are conscious of the choices they make and the consequences of those decisions,
- think with their heart as well as their mind, and
- learn from their mistakes.

Law 4. Least Effort

People who comprehend least effort

- work smarter, not harder;
- use failure or upsetting experiences as opportunities for creative responses; and
- practice the art of defenselessness.

(Continued)

(Continued)

Law 5. Intention and Desire

People who incorporate intention and desire

- put their attention on the present and their intention on the future,
- are aware of their desires and make plans to realize them, and
- relinquish attachment to specific outcomes and allow for unanticipated outcomes.

Law 6. Detachment

People who practice detachment

- accept the illusion of security,
- are willing to step into the unknown, and
- are open to all possibilities.

Law 7. Dharma or Purpose in Life

People who find dharma or purpose in life

- embrace their personal uniqueness,
- discover their unique talents as well as their unique needs, and
- serve others.

---

vision to encourage children to develop efficacious behaviors. Pure potentiality begins with practicing silence or meditation. We all feel better when we are able to build in "me time" where we are alone with ourselves, preferably with our conscious thoughts tuned out. Finding a calm inner space not only nurtures wholeness and self-awareness, it is relevant for individuals with learning differences who experience high anxiety. We will consider the benefits of meditation in Chapter Eight.

The simple act of giving requires no more for persons with learning differences than anyone else. Many states have incorporated service learning into the curriculum. Opportunities to get involved in the community make the playing field level for children and adults with learning differences. Students are honored at graduation for their service; adults gain positive recognition for civic involvement. We know of no communities without opportunities to volunteer. How many times have we heard that giving is its own reward? Parents and teachers who model giving, not only with their greater community but in their interactions with children and students, will pass on an essential element of feeling good about oneself and one's place in the world.

Although *karma* conjures images of 1960s hippies or ascetic monks, it affects all our lives in a simple manner. Any decision or choice we make will have consequences. It's that simple. Difficulties understanding cause and effect figure into many types of learning differences. An improved understanding benefits academic comprehension; social interactions; and a clearer sense of accountability, responsibility, and autonomy. A corollary of karma appears in almost every major religion and countless approaches to counseling: "Think with your

> ### Henry's Story
>
> Personal experience has given us a deeply personal appreciation of practicing the art of defenselessness.
>
> My role as a dean meant working with students, faculty, administrators, and parents who were angry or upset. For various reasons, they blamed the dean. Chopra would say they were not taking responsibility for their own feelings, but we cannot control how others feel. Initially, I would push back. After coming across the art of defenselessness, I began to practice it. People tended to back off their anger if they did not meet resistance. Responding with, "I can understand how you feel about this and how I may have upset you" rather than "You're wrong. I did/didn't do that" diffused confrontational situations. It also provided the opportunity to look for common ground, perhaps the best way to begin the search for a solution.

heart as well as your head." This axiom zeroes in on the human and personal implications of our choices, asking us to use empathic emotional resources as part of the thinking process.

Intention and Desire underlies the concept of having goals, planning for them, and allowing goals to morph. Students with learning differences want validation of their dreams and desires, as do all students. Desire without action leads only to unfulfilled dreams. Adults should help students to articulate goals and guide them toward matching goals with strengths. Learning how to analyze goals and create a series of steps to reach them are equally important. The journey will not be smooth, but those who are willing to leave the beaten path may find a meaningful new direction. A rigid adherence to a linear journey is more likely to lead to frustration and dissatisfaction. Albert Einstein reputedly said, "Stupidity is doing the same thing over and over again but expecting different results." Persistence needs to be tempered with flexibility. Teachers and parents have opportunities to facilitate the acquisition of these qualities.

Intention and Desire organically connects to the sixth law of *Detachment*. Chopra continues with the previous theme of relinquishing attachment to specific outcomes and allowing for unanticipated outcomes. This precept transforms the aphorism of "If at first you don't succeed, try, try again" to "If at first you don't succeed, try something different." The divergent thinking style of many children and adults with learning differences, discussed earlier in this chapter, comes into play as a positive force for finding new and creative solutions when others do not work.

The seventh and concluding law of *Dharma or Purpose in Life* speaks directly to individuals with learning differences. A tenet of theory and practice in education is to help students with learning differences understand their own learning styles and capitalize on their strengths. In addition, the precept of service returns us to the importance of giving. Karma aside, serving others makes people feel good about themselves. Virtually all religions promote serving humanity and the greater good. It is spiritually and personally fulfilling. Overlooking service opportunities takes away a critical opportunity to find meaningfulness, satisfaction, and a sense of contentment in adult life. No matter what our individual strengths and weaknesses are, we are all gifted with the ability to give.

SUMMARY AND SYNTHESIS OF MODELS OF SUCCESS

The recommendations for successful life outcomes from these different perspectives are remarkably similar and consistent. Their confluence creates a holistic sense of success in its broadest sense—a meaningful, purposeful, and satisfying adulthood. The similarities of these models or perspectives on success support their credibility. Equally important, they speak directly to facilitating a successful transition to adulthood for students with learning differences.

These perspectives embrace the importance of knowing, understanding, and behaving in accordance with one's true self. The literature on learning differences has emphasized an awareness of personal strengths and weaknesses. The process may be external, such as using testing and specific educational and social experience to generate self-understanding. It may also be internal through exercises such as reflection and meditation. This movement toward autonomy leads to a better sense of personal accountability and to responsibly responding to consequences of one's behavior. Goal planning becomes efficacious when it is connected to a sense of strengths, weaknesses, and needs. Meaningful, realistic, and sequential goals create the motivation necessary to persist. Self-actualization also creates the understanding of our limitations in controlling external events. It allows us to seek balance and embrace a variety of salutary experiences.

Complementing this focus on self is the intentional effort to understand other viewpoints and work cooperatively and interdependently. The ability to take another's perspective is in part developmental; we generally see this attribute take root in adolescence. It communicates respect for others. We cannot assume that students with learning disabilities will simply mature into empathetic and altruistic adults. We need to adopt approaches to build these skills. Whether it be a boss, employee, client, friend, or a significant other, respect builds trust and mutual respect. Projecting positivity adds to the mix. People gravitate to positive individuals much more easily than to negative ones. However, if these traits are not genuine, they will ultimately fail. Encouraging and teaching proactive social skills is essential to positive outcomes. Positive social interactions are inherently rewarding. The more adults with learning differences embrace thoughtful, honest, and respectful social interactions, the more they will practice these effective behaviors.

We place a special emphasis on a desire to give and offer service. As we have said, this levels the playing field for adults with learning differences. Helping others in need, directly or indirectly, takes us away from the problems of our own lives. It is the best antidote for almost any negative psychological state. We reaffirm an essential component of our humanness. We succeed when we touch another's life.

WHAT IS SUCCESS IN ADULTHOOD?

Success is related to positive careers, interpersonal satisfaction, and a general sense of meaningfulness or purpose in life. As a conclusion to this chapter, let's reframe the notion of successfully transitioning students with learning differences to adulthood to a focus on how to help our children and students become happy when they are adults. After all, manifestations of success do not mean much if an individual is not happy or content at some level.

We allow money and acquisitions to drive our sense of being happy yet we are surprised and disappointed when they do not lead to happiness. We look to interpersonal relationships to fulfill many needs. Although strong and loving interpersonal relationships may be a component of happiness, having close bonds does not preclude sadness, a lack of purpose, and a general sense of being untethered.

A relatively recent field, sometimes termed *the sociology of happiness*, explores the underpinnings of why some people tend to be happy while others do not. Happiness is a little like jazz: We have trouble defining it, but we know it when he hear it. "Feeling good—enjoying life and wanting that feeling to be maintained" (Layard, 2005, p. 12) characterizes happiness in a general sense but does not address how one develops happiness. A more nuanced construct envisions happiness as comprising "positive moods and emotions, but it includes 'mood propensities' as well. A happy person on this account is one who finds it (relatively) easy to experience positive moods and emotions, one whose experience of life amounts to 'psychic affirmation'" (Haybron, 2008).

In *The Pursuit of Unhappiness: The Elusive Psychology of Well-Being* (2008), Daniel Haybron argues that most people do not have an accurate sense of how they feel, sentimentalize past circumstances, fool themselves into thinking that they were happy, misinterpret what made them happy, and, consequently, make poor decisions that result in the opposite outcome. Being accurately in touch with our feelings should lead to better choices. We need to have greater clarity about our emotional states and pursue situations that are congruent. We also would do well to tone down our expectations of being able to create happiness no matter the circumstance. A sense of entitlement to being happy pervades much of our culture. The adage "the grass is always greener on the other side of the pasture" speaks to the elusive nature of happiness.

We have all heard stories about adult millennials who reject the workplace as it is. They want to determine their own hours, how much they can work from home, how they dress at work, and even what recreational activities are available from their employer. The older generation may find this sense of entitlement unacceptable and perhaps bizarre. Haybron might dismiss this attitude as a precursor to unhappiness. Ironically, companies are increasingly accommodating this new approach to a working life. Apparently, productivity increases when employees are happy.

Opportunities to find different kinds of work environments are increasing. It is eminently sensible to find a work environment that fits with an understanding of what makes us happy. For some individuals, working in a more independent, schedule-free environment may be a perfect fit. However, many adults with learning differences will not fare so well in this free-for-all non-workplace workplace. For adults with learning differences, issues with organization and time management may overwhelm the freedom of an unstructured workplace. For those who already feel socially isolated, working solitarily from home intensifies loneliness. Environments with structure and opportunities for personal interactions for these individuals may be beneficial. Self-awareness is more than identifying strengths and weaknesses. People who have strong self-awareness recognize their emotional state and what effect the emotion will have.

Ultimately, happiness is a deeply internal and personal construct. In spite of our culture's preoccupation with rugged individualism, as social creatures, we will do better by trying to locate and nurture our place in the world. Philosophers and researchers have attempted to wrestle with this idea in countless ways over millennia. Of all the models of successful life outcomes, *Tuesdays With Morrie* has resonated with legions of readers in a deeply intimate way (Albom, 1997). We conclude this chapter with our synthesis of Morrie's life to-do list:

- ☐ Love your family and connect with others to love and care about.
- ☐ Find a career that has meaning for you.
- ☐ Contribute to the greater good of your community.

In our experience, no one will go wrong checking the boxes on this list.

4 Success and Outcomes of Adults With Learning Differences

I think I identify with people in low self-esteem positions or people who are struggling to believe in themselves because I had that experience so intimately.

—Ken Druck, eminent grief counselor and author

Early research on adults with disabilities, which largely did not start until the 1980s, tended to highlight difficulties and dysfunction. However, adults with learning differences have also managed adult demands adeptly and successfully. Many of the factors contributing to successful adult outcomes are variable rather than fixed. Put another way, we can teach students with learning differences to acquire attributes that improve the likelihood of a successful and satisfying adult life, but the result is not a given. We will explore Ray Peterson's story and consider where things may have gone wrong. We will then present positive outcomes and use them as a starting point for teaching for the lifespan.

Ray's story is typical of a kind of life outcome that occurs when normal adult development collides with the nuances associated with learning differences. Ray Peterson was angry at the world. In his early twenties and struggling to find a job, he'd had a tough time at school, where he was teased because of his learning differences. He did not make friends easily and, without meaning to, did and said things that did not make him popular. Too much activity in the environment easily overwhelmed him, from doing work in class to playing basketball to hanging out with a group of kids.

Ray was fascinated with geeky gadgets and thought it would be cool to work in a Best Buy type of store. He saw an opening at a local store and showed up to apply. The first thing they asked him to do was fill out an application. Ray didn't write well and had poor handwriting, so he told the receptionist he didn't like the idea of filling out the form. He waited to be called. Fifteen minutes went by. It was twenty minutes before he was asked to come in, and as he walked by the manager into the office, he made sure to point out that he was angry because he had been kept waiting. When Ray did not get the job, he could not figure out why he had not made the right impression. He concluded once again that the world was against him. He carried a chip on his shoulder that made failure a self-fulfilling prophecy.

Regardless whether studies point to negative or positive outcomes, specifics of Ray's learning differences persisted into adulthood. Learning differences are a risk factor that increases the likelihood of poor life-adjustment skills, inadequate social graces, and insufficient workplace readiness (Morrison & Cosden, 1997). Even successful adults have reported that difficulties in areas such as reading, writing, and math continue and often impact work, but they generally have found ways to compensate. Many are not comfortable about disclosing their learning differences in the workplace.

As we discussed in Chapter 2, the effects of learning differences in adults range from the general arc of their lives to relationships and performing everyday tasks. Problems with overall organization, time management, prioritizing, planning, anticipating outcomes, and so on create formidable challenges for many adults with learning differences.

NEW PERSPECTIVES

It would be easy to write about all the bad things that can happen to adults with disabilities. Exploring the *what*s and *why*s of negative outcomes has some merit, especially if such knowledge can help teachers better prepare their students for the adult world. However, learning from adults who have been successful offers better models, practices, and perspectives than using stories of failure.

A theoretical context that arose in the late 1980s was the phenomenon of risk and resilience. As we have discussed, adults with learning differences are more at risk for setbacks. However, many demonstrate a resilience that allows them to work through their struggles. For example, problems with finances do not have to be insurmountable and result in a general downward spiral. Using software or finding outside support may alleviate most of these concerns. Many of us are overwhelmed by doing our taxes. Going it alone can cause overwhelming stress and lead to potential financial disaster. On the other hand, software (such as Quicken) or tax preparation services take away most of the pain. For those who can afford it, a certified public accountant offers a tremendously secure manner of accomplishing this task. Resilience may not involve so much intestinal fortitude as simply making a practical decision on how to solve a problem.

As teachers and parents, we need to make our students aware of this type of support, but awareness may not be enough. Individuals with learning differences may be reluctant to take advantage of support. If they no longer wish to be identified as having a disability, they will not seek services. Consequently, transition strategies must involve getting students to buy into using available supports, from academic to basic adult needs, when they have proven to be helpful.

Many adults with learning differences wind up somewhere in the middle. They learn to cope and compensate but realize that the persistent difficulties continue to make life difficult and frustrating. They accomplish more than they might have anticipated, but they still feel held back. Emma Bixler, a dyslexic adult, writes movingly of both her triumphs and tribulations of making it as a young adult (Bixler, 2014). She reminds us that self-acceptance may be more important that any material manifestation of success:

Recently I was typing a document proposing a job position at a non-profit I've worked with in the past. Here I am: a 25-year-old, B.A. holding, native English speaker, young adult. I sent my document to two friends, asked my partner to read it over if he had time, and sent it to my mom, who has filled in as my personal editor since the day I was expected to write. No one responded. I was impeding their lives, asking them to take time out of their day to focus on my needs. I read the document over again and again, printed it out and followed each letter with the tip of my pencil, closed the door and read it out loud to the wall, who listened so intensely and yet stayed silent when I asked for feedback. Each letter stared back at me in the black and white with which it was printed. Mistakes? I didn't know. My pencil, the wall, my eyes, did not inform me of any. Time on my end was running out. I had promised to send in the document that day, and it was already noon. Ok, so maybe I had asked everyone only the night before and should have asked a few days before if I was really on my game, which I usually am not . . . when faced with writing a document, I spend half of the time before the deadline putting my hands to my face, pulling them

(Continued)

(Continued)

down and taking in deep long breaths and then throwing out any tai chi calm I create by asking, "Why?! Why me?!" and firmly focusing on the big orange negative letters that seem to hover above my forehead - "CAN'T, I can't do this." I read the document one more time. Time has run out. I click send and with it release the anxiety that has been building up in me since I realized that not being able to read, write, and spell comes with a heavy stigma I have to carry around. I open a tab to the internet and get lost with any rambling wonderings I find there. I get a response from the non-profit. It's positive. They like it. They want to move forward. They were impressed with my ideas. Orange letters of "I can't" are washed away by calming blue waves - "CAN, I can."

Three hours later, my mother replies to the email, "Quick, don't send it in yet! You meant "personnel", not "personal", right?!" Those orange letters come right back, smacking me in my face.

The frustration, struggle, and loneliness didn't evaporate when I graduated from school. As much as school was the enemy, in hindsight, it was a safe haven where structure was set up to admit that I was dyslexic, admit that I am dyslexic. I know how alone it feels to graduate high school and still struggle. And how awkward the same struggles feel in new environments. How I still feel the panic from when my teacher would walk up and down the aisles watching us write down our answers. Only now it's my boss who comes up behind me, asking me to change the wording in a document and watching me stumble. Red squiggles pointing to where I need to fix something, she interjects, "That's an 'a'. Oh, and there is an 'ee'. Emma, there are really only three letters in that word," not the nine extra I nervously added as I quickly tried to sound out the word in my head. My boss's pointing just adds to my stress, elongating the red squiggly lines filling the whole page. I come home exhausted from trying to shield myself from the familiar ache of feeling stupid, but now I lie there alone, no dorm room full of endless friends to support me or a house full of family who ache with me. Now I lie in bed alone, the few friends, who live nearby, busy with their own adult lives.

I have graduated from school and now I am left in the dark. There is no deadline from the disabilities office to push me into explaining, educating, or even casually dropping that I am dyslexic and therefore need the following accommodations to succeed. I have no neatly packaged accommodations to hand over to my boss as a set of instructions on how to work with me. Instead, I'm left with the conversation, just my boss and me, and the looming thought that my boss, unlike my teachers and professors, has the ability to tell me, "All those red squiggles don't have a place in this office."

So what happens after school?

This is what happens after school.

I am still dyslexic.

Parents, go home, and drop any hope that your dyslexic child will be fixed. Realize that is ok. Because in thinking that they can be fixed, you are telling them that they are broken. Sure, the endless hours of tutoring I spent growing up have allowed me to touch the tip of the phonetic iceberg, but I am still lost at sea, floating among letters that seem to squish together, their sounds lost among the waves.

All the while they were teaching me how to sound out letters, no one told me how heavy the stigma of having a disability weighs. Between learning all the letter combinations that make the long 'o' sound, none of my teachers paused to explain how the only thing I would need to overcome is others' assumptions of me, not my own dyslexia. While practicing saying words while my tutor covered up the first letter leaving me to read the new word that was left on the page, she never once mentioned how the obstacles that would come up in my life would not be due to my own inabilities but due to the lack of education and understanding of others. As I sat next to my mom and dad at IEP meetings, staring blankly as they talked with all the professionals in my life, no one interrupted to explain to me that when I attended a conference on dyslexia in 2014 all my negative emotions would come flooding back when meeting parents who shared with me the same misguidance my parents experienced in 1994, "Dyslexia? Oh, we don't use that word." And no one told me that what really would hold me back was not my inabilities to read, write, or spell but my anger, my emotions, and my frustrations of never being allowed to own my own identity.

I am dyslexic.

Approaching dyslexia with the mindset of needing to be fixed leaves a gap in the dyslexic community, dyslexic adults. Dyslexic adults are missing because parents, educators, professionals, and researchers aren't letting our dyslexic children grow up to be dyslexic. Dyslexics are held back by a sliver of hope that one day they will be normal, that one day they won't have to live in the fear of being found out as stupid, that one day they will be fixed. Trapped in this hope, parents, teachers, and professionals hold out the promise of an easy life that comes with becoming normal, the promise that hard work, effort, and lots of tutoring will allow your child to become successful, achieve whatever they want, overcome their obstacles, and be normal. Normal is easy. Dyslexia is not. What happens when your child isn't fixed, when life is still hard because reading, writing, and spelling are still littered with endless challenges that may get easier but are still firmly placed in the way? Your child will not be fixed. Your child will one day grow up to be a dyslexic adult.

I am a dyslexic adult.

I am looking for my people, my community to acknowledge that I am still here, that we are still here. I am doing now what should have been done in my education starting when I was first diagnosed. I'm embracing who I am. Along with all the tools of being able to sound out words, read more fluently, and write whatever is on my mind, I also should have been given tools to understand the feelings of oppression and discrimination so that I could navigate my feelings with more ease. Instead of feeding my parents with the notion that one day I would be able to spell simple words with ease, educators and professionals should have been supporting my parents' natural inclination to support my own identity.

When we look at the dyslexic child only through an educational lens, we are only seeing half of them. Forgotten are the needs of their emotional wellbeing and their identity. Forgotten is that they are and will always be dyslexic.

ACCENTUATE THE POSITIVE

Best practices should result from a focus on what individuals with learning differences can do rather than on what they cannot. Persons with learning differences excel in virtually every field of human endeavor. We do not need to tout the achievements of famous historical figures, whose learning differences are, at best, anecdotal. We have plenty of success stories in front of our faces. Some of those are well-known personalities who have become famous in entertainment, sports, and business. Henry Winkler (the "Fonz"), Michael Phelps, and Sir Richard Branson, to name a few, provide plenty of evidence through their firsthand accounts of growing up with learning differences and continuing to face and cope with them in adult life. These celebrities have helped raised awareness and present a positive face to a phenomenon that so many of us have viewed negatively and skeptically. They are inspiring role models for everyone. Many of the skills they have developed are attainable. Nevertheless, they have achieved a level of success that is rare and improbable. We can dream of being the best in the world, but that distinction is bestowed only on a relative handful of individuals.

Equally inspiring, and perhaps more practical, are the accomplishments of countless individuals with learning differences who are successful business people (from entrepreneurs to CEOs), respected educators of all stripes, doctors and professionals in all medical services, and individuals dedicated to services ranging from the law to social justice. Add to this successful men and women who are not high-profile professionals but our neighbors and friends who have satisfying careers and jobs, make and maintain personal relationships and friendships, and are active in their communities. They live good lives, and they continue to live with their learning differences. Their levels of success are linked to their coping mechanisms; more successful adults develop better coping mechanisms than those who are less successful. Research in many different fields is helping us discover keys to successful adult outcomes relevant to individuals with learning differences. Moreover, it is clear that individuals can learn to acquire and utilize these practices. Beginning this process in school greatly enhances the likelihood of successful outcomes for our students.

Thomas West's *In the Mind's Eye* (2009) sees a future where the ability to think conceptually and visually may be become more important than communicating through the written word. The age of apps is already upon us, where handheld devices can convert text to speech and follow voice commands. The world of the web lends itself more naturally to right-brain, creative, and nonlinear thinking. In a language-dependent society where linear thinking has been the norm, people with learning differences have been at a significant disadvantage. We have been living in a left-brain world. In the new world of technology, many people with learning differences may have an advantage. We can only hope so. Nevertheless, we still have a ways to go before we can appreciate and fully understand how the world is changing and what lies ahead for adults with learning differences.

FOCUSING ON SUCCESS

Speaking for Themselves proved to be something of a revelation. Clearly, as earlier research had demonstrated, many individuals with learning differences struggled in adulthood. Some of the participants matched the profile of those who were the least well-adjusted. Their difficulties with learning impinged on their ability to lead successful lives. Their education had been limited; they did not go to college. Their learning differences often undermined problem solving, decision making, planning goals, and understanding the complexi-

---

Henry's Story, Part 1

More than twenty years ago, I had the privilege of working with Dr. Paul Gerber, who had been my mentor in graduate school. We set out in 1986 to hear the narratives of adults with learning disabilities. We knew that no single interview could ever uncover all the complex layers that make up adulthood for anyone. Instead, we focused on several domains of adulthood: educational, vocational, social/emotional, daily living, and keys to successful adjustment. We developed an ethnographic interview protocol, where we would encourage the interviewee to be expansive, broad, and reflective. Through this process, we would see the world through their eyes.

We were able to enlist nine adults with learning disabilities to participate in our project, which resulted in the book, *Speaking for Themselves: Ethnographic Interviews With Adults With Learning Disabilities* (Gerber & Reiff, 1991). These adults with learning disabilities seemed to group into three clusters of overall adaptation to adult life as defined by our domains.

Three of our participants were highly adapted (successful professional careers, personal contentment, and well-being), three were moderately adapted, and three were struggling. We were intrigued by the possible reasons for these differences in outcomes. In general, those having the most difficulty had the most severe learning disabilities and residual issues. We cannot really change these types of traits. It was clear that the severity of the disability had an impact, but it was not the sole factor.

Why do some individuals develop better coping mechanisms than others? Alterable variables, the stuff of nurture rather than nature, are the underlying forces in teaching and learning. Do successful adults with learning differences have a different set of learned attributes, characteristics from both their child and adolescent development as well as behaviors learned and utilized in the adult world?

---

ties of independent living in the adult world. Social skills were elusive, and they found themselves in similar positions to what previous research had described. They were lonely, isolated, and alienated and did not have a sense of why they found their lives unsatisfactory. They were mired in the low self-concept from their negative experiences in childhood.

Could these outcomes have been different? If these individuals had received better support at home and in school and grown up with a better sense of how to cope and compensate, they likely would have fared better. They might have achieved a higher level of education, one of the most significant factors in career success. They might have had a better sense of themselves as whole persons instead of feeling broken. They might have been able to learn how to form more meaningful interpersonal relationships.

The young adults who were moderately adjusted had fared better in all these areas. They had developed a measure of self-advocacy skills and coping mechanisms for their work. For example, a young man who had worked as both a waiter and electrician created codes for writing down and reading information by substituting numbers to replace much of his writing. He had asked his employers to work with his systems. They complied, largely because he worked hard, was conscientious, and proved his worth as a good employee. He had a positive outlook and was setting goals for his future.

The highly adjusted adults were the most intriguing. They had extended their education to graduate school. They had succeeded as professionals and created fulfilling relationships and personal lives yet they were adamant that their learning differences continued to affect them. They developed creative and highly effective coping strategies at work and at home. For example, one participant had acute difficulties with short-term memory. If she put something in a drawer or cabinet in her kitchen, she would forget where she put it. In order to overcome this issue, she kept virtually everything in view, hanging many implements on the wall and placing others in open cabinets. Her kitchen was not a mess but rather an organized display of what she required to store, cook, and clean. She had trouble reading maps and following directions. In order to drive to a new location and arrive on time, she would practice the route. Street signs and left or right turns were not of much help. Instead, she created a visual route, where she used buildings or landmarks to guide her.

These types of strategies required more work. The successful adults with learning differences had accepted the fact that they would need to work hard—very hard—to manage their lives successfully. A strong work ethic served them extremely well, especially in school and in their careers. They worked harder than their classmates and colleagues. They beat the odds. In addition, the more successfully adapted adults had supportive parents and spouses. Factors such as severity are immutable, but coping strategies can be learned and taught.

Perhaps the future is not as bleak for many adults with learning differences as previous research has suggested. Learning differences from childhood persist, but they do not always preclude the ability to move through adult development in a successful manner.

It was time for a different focus on adult outcomes of adults with learning differences. Successful adults were not only inspirational role models; their paths to success could provide a model for students and young adults with learning differences. Analyzing how they became successful could provide ideas about how to work with children to increase the likelihood of positive outcomes later in life.

STORIES OF SUCCESS

Coller, who was interviewed in *Exceeding Expectations*, is a respected dermatologist. She practices privately and consults. She relates personally to her patients. In addition to her skills as a practitioner, she has a wonderful bedside manner.

Henry's Story, Part 2

The reasonable path to explore our questions was to identify a larger group of successful adults with learning disabilities and conduct similar but more comprehensive interviews. Additionally, an expanded interview would address the intersection of learning disabilities and success, probing the reasons why these individuals had accomplished so much.

Our research efforts led to more than seventy in-depth ethnographic interviews with successful adults with learning disabilities. The resulting book, *Exceeding Expectations: Successful Adults With Learning Disabilities* (Reiff, Gerber, & Ginsberg, 1997), described and analyzed these interviews. A notable contribution from our research was the attempt to explain how and why these individuals had become so successful. A comprehensive qualitative analysis revealed that seven attributes (we termed them *internal decision-making* and *external manifestations*) generally distinguished adults who were successful from those who weren't. We conceptualized the seven attributes as *alterable variables*, meaning that they could be taught and learned, and used them to create a vocational model of success for adults with learning disabilities. Success in adult life is relatively predictable and not primarily a matter of luck or preexisting circumstances.

Exceeding Expectations presented personal stories of success. Careers of participants included law, medicine, higher education, and, especially, business. Many of the successful business people were entrepreneurs, a nod to the creativity that is often associated with learning differences.

Life was not easy growing up. She is severely dyslexic. She was able to fake her way through her early elementary years by memorizing words and even whole stories. When called upon to read, she recited from memory rather than actually reading the text. We often hear that in the early grades, children learn to read but as time goes on, they read to learn. Coller's luck had run out. Memorizing words would not help her with assignments centered on reading and writing. She began to fail. She felt stupid.

Her father, a highly respected doctor, and her mother expected that she would be a successful student and adult. Fortunately, her parents, especially her mother, began to understand why Coller was having such trouble. Seeing her at home and watching her understand and solve problems, sometimes in unusual ways, her parents had no doubt that she was a bright child. She was obviously capable, but school was destroying her self-esteem. She had severe difficulties with reading and writing. Otherwise, she was precocious and capable.

Some of her teachers were supportive. The powerful impact of teachers lasts a lifetime. Great teachers can be mentors and role models. We may remember a moment in class or a conversation outside that has helped steer us and even comfort us as we took on the demands of adulthood. A great teacher boosts self-confidence and makes students feel capable of meeting new challenges.

Some of her teachers were downright cruel. One cutting comment or biting criticism can undermine all the positive messages a child has heard elsewhere, especially if another adult does not step in to help that child regroup and persevere. Coller found herself in a vicious cycle. Some of her teachers told her she was lazy, stupid, or both. She started acting out and attracting negative attention. She built a new persona. She preferred being known as *bad* rather than *dumb*. Her teachers saw her behavior as another example of her inability to handle school.

Coller's mother was her saving grace. She reinforced Coller's ability, her "specialness." She told Coller not to listen to those teachers who ceaselessly criticized her. "Don't worry so much about reading and writing. Someday, you will have a secretary who will do those things for you." As Coller fondly recalls, she did not really know what a secretary was. But it sounded good. The idea was reassuring.

Nonetheless, her parents did not accept that she would fail at school. They bore down and persuaded—maybe even forced—her to work hard. She had tutoring after school, often with an aunt. She attended summer school. She did not like it, but she persevered. Her grades got better. She made it through high school and graduated from college. As she delved into subject areas of more personal interest, her engagement increased and she became more proficient. Medical school had seemed a stretch, but coming from a family of doctors increased her determination. In medical school, she intentionally specialized in dermatology because the textbooks relied heavily on pictures while having less reading than other areas. She was able to process and understand the information. Coller explained that compared to some other areas of medicine, dermatology is more visual and concrete.

As a successful doctor, she still needs to put in extra effort. She rises as early as 4:00 a.m. to read medical journals, as doctors are required to do. The reading is painfully slow. She does enough to keep up with the ever-changing demands of medicine. She has to be a more intuitive practitioner. In so many ways, her style has become an advantage.

In their book, *The Dyslexic Advantage*, Brock and Fernette Eide (2011) chronicle the lives of many successful individuals with dyslexia. These individuals demonstrate strengths that were nurtured but largely unrecognized in school. The Eides use the acronym *MIND* to capture the unique strengths of individuals with dyslexia. In some instances, these same strengths can interfere with reading letters and numbers while simultaneously allowing for extraordinary capabilities that those without dyslexia often do not have to the same degree. The MIND strengths are **m**aterial reasoning, **i**nterconnected reasoning, **n**arrative reasoning, and **d**ynamic reasoning. Malcolm Gladwell's *David and Goliath* (2013) even promotes the idea of a "desirable difficulty," such as dyslexia. It makes reading and writing frustrating but, at the same time, may force dyslexic individuals to develop better listening and more creative problem-solving skills. As we mentioned earlier, *In the Mind's Eye* not only promotes the concept of the "gifted dyslexic" but explores a right-brain advantage in an increasingly right-brain world.

Steven Spielberg is one of the most famous dyslexics. In an interview with Quinn Bradlee (2012), he shares how he followed his passion, took advantage of his strengths, and reframed his dyslexia into a useful skill in the film industry. As with many persons of his generation, he was not diagnosed in school and only recently became aware of why reading has been so difficult and slow. His experiences as a child mirror the feelings of being different and not knowing why.

By the time he was in fourth grade, he was reading at a second-grade level. Some of his teachers thought he was lazy. Some equated his reading and writing difficulties with a lack of intelligence, although it is difficult to imagine not being able to see his creativity, imagination, and sharp mind. As with persons such as Coller, his parents did not accept that he was not bright and reinforced his intelligence and creativity.

He had a circle of friends who were like him—smart but not particularly successful in school. Schoolmates saw them as geeks, but they were okay with being different. They tended to develop different passions and followed them.

We all know Spielberg's passion. He wanted to make films. His parents supported him, bought him an eight millimeter camera, and assisted his early projects—usually filming in the desert. Part of what drove Spielberg to make movies was his desire to create his own universe, especially one in which he would be in control. As arguably the most successful director in history, his films have spanned an enormous breadth of styles and subjects. Many but not all of his films have created alternate worlds, such as *Close Encounters* and *E.T.* His films often involve an outsider who is doubted and even maligned at first but who succeeds at finding a larger truth.

Spielberg also has recognized his dyslexia advantage. It takes him two to three times as long to read a script as a typical director. But his painstaking approach yields a deeper understanding and helps him internalize the script early on. He visualizes characters, places, and the arc of the story. He will certainly be remembered for the breathtaking visuals in so many of his films.

We caution against assuming that any kid with learning differences can grow up to be an Oscar-winning director. Success is relative. The key issue is to unlock potential, provide support, and find environments that give children with learning differences opportunities to succeed as adults. The research is clear. Unemployment and underemployment are not inevitable outcomes. Personal satisfaction, a sense of purpose, and finding meaningfulness in life can be fostered in childhood.

K–12 education is ultimately concerned with preparing students academically, intellectually, vocationally, socially/emotionally, and even morally for the rest of their lives. Familiarity with research exploring implications of learning differences in late adolescence and adulthood is critical for secondary (if not all) teachers. A focus on transition planning for students entering postsecondary education and/or the workplace has become part of educational practice and policy. Teachers fail their students if they do not prepare them for adulthood. Lifespan preparation should be the core of curriculum and instruction. Having an overall sense of fulfillment as an adult requires the ability to function effectively in many areas.

PART II
Good Teaching

How do we teach skills that children will use in adulthood to help them accomplish what they set out to do? Two distinct but overlapping sets of attributes form the basis of this pedagogy: those from the realm of cognitive skills, traditionally associated with academic performance and achievement, and those from the world of emotional intelligence, our ability to use emotions to mediate our approaches and reactions to life around and within us. In both of these areas, executive functioning or metacognition allows us to be aware of who we are and how to approach situations through planning, prioritizing, controlling impulses, managing time, organizing, and self-monitoring. It is the basis for directing and evaluating our thinking processes. Constructive, consistent, and fluent executive functioning and metacognition are the keys to regulating emotions and behaviors. Persons who regulate their emotions and behaviors are more likely to see results that are consistent with their expectations and find greater coherence between their inner sense of self and their interactions with the world around them. They achieve a greater degree of self-actualization.

Years of research have given us a good idea of both the skills and content we need to teach students with learning differences. Additionally, the past thirty years of research on metacognition and executive functioning have provided us with exceptional tools to teach students *how* to learn. However, for students with learning differences, one underpinning to both of these sets of pedagogy is *self-awareness*, a significant developmental construct that is largely ignored in terms of instruction at school.

Many excellent theories and some programs have been designed to promote an understanding of self, self-advocacy, self-determination, and self-efficiency. Yet more than three decades of this work has not produced readily available tools for translating what teachers, parents, and psychologists know about how students cognitively process information to the students themselves. In Part II, we advance our understanding of these models into practical steps that allow teachers, parents, and mentors to teach self-awareness of learning to children.

Self-awareness of learning is specific: It is an understanding of how one's brain works in relation to learning. It is grounded in an understanding of the aspects of cognition and behavior that individuals need in order to learn: auditory working memory, long-term retrieval, verbal fluency, processing speed, visualization, phonology, orthography, executive functions, oral language, nonverbal processing, attention, executive functions, and emotional regulation. Self-awareness of learning is a critical first step in preparing individuals for a lifetime. When we explicitly teach students about learning processes, they will able to recognize their individual strengths and talents. Moreover, self-awareness of learning offers a direction (and in some cases, needed buy in) for the learning methods a teacher might use. It also helps students learn how to learn through metacognition and executive functions. Mather and Tanner write, "[T]the major purpose of assessing cognitive skills is to attempt to explain the student's unique strengths, as well as the factors that contribute to a student's difficulties" (2014, p. 3). We must take our understanding of students' learning processes and engage in the methods that impart self-awareness of learning processes.

We begin Part II of our book with focus on a synthesis of the fifty years of effective instruction from the field of cognition and special education. These chapters embrace the Common Core State Standards and Universal Design for Learning while preserving the continuum of placements and school options for all students. We then turn to the importance of developing affective qualities such as self-understanding, creating relationships, and building self-confidence. The final chapter brings us full circle in our vision to prepare all children to become autonomous individuals who embrace self-advocacy and take proactive approaches. They learn to take control of their lives, the outcome of a successful transition to adulthood.

5 Building a Better Classroom

The best way to inspire people to superior performance is to convince them by everything you do and by your everyday attitude that you are wholeheartedly supporting them.

—Harold S. Geenen

The beginning of the road to successfully transitioning students with learning differences to adulthood starts as early as elementary school. The early years of education focus on building basic skills in reading, writing, math, and social interactions. As we know, students with learning differences often lack some basic skills by the time they enter high school. Without these skills, they are more vulnerable to academic failure, negative outcomes, and a less-than-successful transition to the demands of further education, career, and other realities of adulthood. We need to build a better classroom if we want our children and students to prosper in life.

What does it take to build a better classroom? The classroom is the location of the majority of student-teacher interaction. Classrooms should be designed to maximize performance. An effective classroom is more than a room where instruction and learning occur; it is a flexible control center that maximizes the performance of both teacher and learner. In order for this to happen in practice and not just theory, teachers must first move beyond knowledge of the curriculum to knowledge of individual learning processes. As teachers gain greater knowledge about cognition, feedback loops, learning differences, and different types of instruction, they create opportunities to maximize the performance of learners.

How do teachers tap into this knowledge? The manner and condition in which students learn is often gleaned through a variety of sources. These include for example, psychoeducational evaluations, Individual Education Programs (IEPs), student observations (e.g., error analysis, pencil grip and handwriting, response analysis), and an understanding of a particular diagnosis (if one exists). Once this knowledge is acquired, teachers can effectively operate the classroom's control center. Teachers will be most successful at building this new kind of classroom by clearly communicating these goals to administrators and other teachers who may help to lay the foundation for this new way of conceptualizing the classroom. Some teachers will need to be their own advocates, since it is uncommon practice to attempt to discover *how* a student learns and what *methods of instruction* may work. Resistance to new approaches is to be expected. Even special education teachers can find themselves about to start a school year without access to student records, especially if a teacher is recently hired before the start of the year. In some cases, students' records are simply unavailable, and for other students, there are no records other than report cards and comments. Another way to begin to bridge the gap between the functional impacts of learning differences during the school day is to ask other specialists how different learning modalities relate to the curriculum. For example, a conversation with a district's school psychologist and occupational therapist can reveal how a student's anxiety disorder and fine-motor coordination difficulty (e.g., dysgraphia) will impact math and written expression rather than "He has trouble with handwriting. He just needs occupational therapy." Similarly, a conversation with the school's speech and language pathologist can help a teacher understand why a student diagnosed with an autism spectrum disorder may struggle with reading comprehension and cooperative learning groups. This understanding should lead to different solutions than those offered to a student with, for example, attention deficit/hyperactivity disorder (ADHD). Once this knowledge about the brain and performance is acquired, a better classroom can be built. To be clear, we are not referring to *differentiated instruction*, an approach that diversifies instruction but without a clear grasp of the intersection between the brain and learning.

An understanding about brain-based learning and student performance allows teachers to effectively infuse learning strategies and accommodations into instruction, utilize both low and high technologies, demonstrate critical teaching behaviors (including feedback), and articulate the essential objectives of a lesson. These are all ways to meet the needs of students with a vast array of learning differences in inclusive and self-contained classrooms and maintain high standards. These techniques allow more students with learning differences to remain in and excel in the general education classroom. However, given that 70% of secondary students with learning disabilities comprehend text below basic levels and 77% are below basic levels in their understanding of math application (Cortiella & Horowitz, 2014), we still need a place for basic skill instruction to continue beyond elementary school in order to lay the foundation for successful transitions.

FACING NEW CHALLENGES

One ongoing challenge with any standards-based educational model is that IEP goals are designed to align with grade-level standards, even though many students don't have the skills to attain those standards without well-thought-out support. Secondary students with learning differences have uneven or limited achievement in basic principles of reading, math, and writing. Given that the Common Core State Standards (CCSS) are designed to prepare students for college, individual districts and schools will need to develop systems to ensure that secondary students receive basic skill instruction when needed. Middle and high school teachers are trained to teach subject matter such as science, chemistry, and history and not basic skills. Additionally, for children in resource rooms or special education pull-out or push-in programs, collaboration among all teachers is imperative so that specialized instruction is generalized across all classes and settings. Finally, in this era of tests both teacher created and standardized, accommodations for tests and instruction should be considered for students who need them. As educational systems evolve with Universal Design for Learning (UDL), each of these suggestions will hopefully become part of all classrooms.

We have incorporated these approaches into what we refer to as the MASSive approach to teaching (Ofiesh, 2010). MASSive can be used to troubleshoot educational programs for students with special needs or as a way for teachers to simply consider effective options for students who are struggling to meet the requirements of a standards-based curriculum. The chapter concludes with recommendations from teachers who have made connections between how their curriculum and instruction facilitate successful adult outcomes.

A MULTIFACETED APPROACH TO SCHOOL SUCCESS (MASSive)

The MASSive approach was first developed after years of distilling what middle and high school special education teachers need to know in order to support students with basic skills at fifth-grade levels and below. It is designed so that students at all grade levels meet content standards and make gains in basic skills. For many secondary school teachers, this is a struggle, since content classes make up most of the day. Resource room teachers typically use that time to help students succeed in content courses rather than, for example, teaching students with dyslexia how to read or acquire other basic skills such as written expression.

One way to implement the MASSive approach is to take the annual goal from a student's IEP and generate an idea for each of the areas listed below. In this manner, teachers will end up with a comprehensive approach to learning. For students who are not on 504 plans or IEPs, the MASSive approach can be used to develop an effective plan of support in the general education classroom. MASSive addresses six important areas to meet the needs of students with learning differences. It "waters up" learning, since it is designed to help students stay afloat in general education classes such as history and physics despite having poor, weak, or below-basic

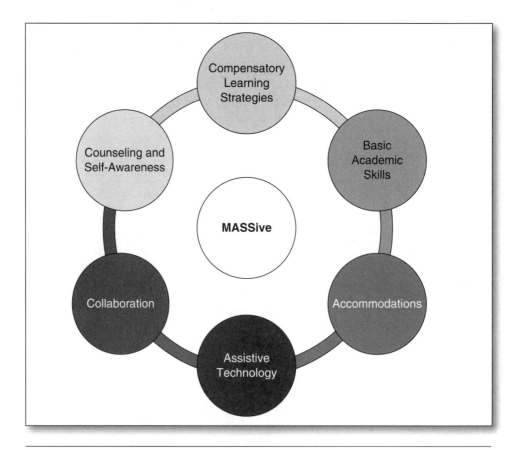

Source: Ofiesh, N. (2010). *MASSive: A multifaceted approach to school success for individuals with learning differences.* Retrieved June 16, 2015, from http://www.nicoleofiesh.com/intervention.html

reading, writing, math, and/or executive function skills. These six areas are for overall consideration for each student; yet few students will need all of the components. The MASSive framework allows teachers to be confident that they have approached ideas for learning support comprehensively.

Compensatory Learning Strategies

When students have difficulty with basic skills such as reading fluently, decoding words, reading comprehension, handwriting, retrieving words fast enough to write sentences for an essay, recalling math facts quickly, or remembering steps to math algorithms, content classes such as English and biology become exceptionally hard to keep up with. Students who fall behind are at risk for academic difficulties throughout high school. The writing and reading demands can be overwhelming despite the fact that the material may indeed be interesting and the student possesses the critical thinking and reasoning skills needed to master the material. Indeed, it is this higher-order thinking that is appropriately targeted for secondary school. For students with learning differences however, the workload becomes twice as much or more than what a teacher may have intended. Subsequently, the first component of the MASSive approach is the development of a learning strategy.

Learning strategies are generally a *metacognitive strategy*, "the self-reflection or 'thinking about thinking' necessary for students to learn effectively" (Jordan, n.d.). "The term 'cognitive strategies' in its simplest form is the use of the mind (cognition) to solve a problem or complete a task" (Jordan, n.d.). The *strategies* are tools to assist students with learning problems.

> Cognitive strategies may also be referred to as procedural facilita-tors (Bereiter & Scardamalia, 1987), procedural prompts (Rosenshine, 1997) or scaffolds (Palincsar & Brown, 1984). . . . Cognitive strategies provide a structure for learning when a task cannot be completed through a series of steps. For example, algorithms in mathematics provide a series of steps to solve a problem. Attention to the steps results in successful completion of the problem. In contrast, reading comprehension, a complex task, is a good example of a task that does not follow a series of steps. (Jordan, n.d.)

The main goal is always to help the student stay on top of the course demands while basic skill remediation is taking place. The compensatory strategy is not a replacement for basic skill instruction. The compensatory strategy answers the question, "How is this student going to get through this ninth-grade class with a fourth-grade reading level?" A learning strategy may be as simple as a concept map or character web that is developed with the student in order to understand text structure and foster comprehension or it may be a method for organization and time management, such as *The Goal Planning Program* (Reiff, Gerber, & Ginsberg, 1997). A broader extension of the application of learning strategy instruction is known as *content enhancement* (Deshler et al., 2001). Content enhancements infuse strategies into content classes in the general education classroom so that all learners benefit from an effective overarching organizational system, advanced organizers, and metacognitive strategies. When inclusive classrooms embed learning strategies and content enhancements, all students receive executive function training, organization, and management skills (Deshler, Ellis, & Lenz, 1996). Not only does this promote individual strengths by helping students to see different ways to approach a task and problem solve, it allows for basic skill remediation to take place in the resource room, through small-group instruction, or through a Response to Intervention (RTI) method.

Basic Academic Skill Instruction

Large numbers of students with learning differences are not identified as needing specialized services until third grade or later. Many others struggle but not severely enough to receive special education services. Basic skill remediation addresses instruction in reading, writing, and math skills aligned with elementary school standards. After elementary school, no curriculum standards focus on basic skills. Students are expected to move toward standards-based general education curriculum with support only via accommodations and technology. Special education instruction often changes in secondary schools from remediation to content support or a study skills type of format in order to help accomplish this task. However, without learning how to effectively read, write, and understand basic math, secondary students with learning differences are at great risk for dropout or failure (Newman, Wagner, Cameto, Knokey, & Shaver, 2010).

The typical school day in the secondary school does not include many options to provide effective remediation. When strategies are included for all students in the general education classroom, students with below-basic skills can benefit from a secondary resource class that targets individual needs. The What Works Clearinghouse, housed by the Institute of Education Sciences (http://ies.ed.gov/ncee/wwc/) provides information to teachers and administrators on hundreds of research-based programs designed to improve basic skills. These reports allow educators to determine whether certain programs have been effective with secondary students as well as the time demands required to make performance gains.

Technology is now one of the most powerful tools for implementing basic skill remediation in the school day as long as teachers carry out an intervention with the precision needed to make a significant difference. One reading program developed by Mindplay, Inc.—Mindplay Virtual Reading Coach—offers one of the most highly scaffolded and intuitive reading intervention programs available. The program is presented entirely online with embedded videos of teachers for each lesson. Multiple layers of assessment and feedback allow for effective instruction without overwhelming the teacher with time-consuming record keeping.

Some may be aghast at the idea of having classroom teachers replaced with online instruction, but the competing demands of content support and basic skill support provide for the appropriate use of technology. Moreover, researchers at the University of Arizona have found that students with learning differences and in Title 1 programs can make significant gains in ten months by working with Mindplay Virtual Reading Coach four days a week, thirty minutes each day, with most achieving grade-level reading abilities. This process leaves time for resource and secondary teachers to focus on learning strategies and standards-based curriculum while staying committed to providing basic skill instruction. In our version of a better classroom, all teachers can create space in the day for students to receive basic skill remediation and incorporate learning strategies for content instruction.

Assistive Technology

Technology is a broad notion. Assistive technology (AT) was originally designed to assist individuals to do a variety of tasks. Over time, these devices, such as audio-based texts that were originally developed for individuals with dyslexia and blindness, have become desirable to many individuals. Along the lines of UDL, AT devices can be used in the classroom for all students in a variety of ways. Students can use these technological tools to make learning more efficient. Let's take a look at how this can fit into the MASSive approach. A student who has difficulty recalling basic math facts quickly can be taught a compensatory learning strategy such as Touch Math, but the same student may also participate in an individualized math program such as enVision Math to help with basic skill remediation and use technology in the form of a calculator to develop knowledge of advanced math concepts such as algebra.

AT devices may actually function as a compensatory strategy or an accommodation. Consideration of AT is nonetheless one aspect of the MASSive approach because, as within the IEP process, AT in and of itself should be evaluated with respect to how it can help students with their individual needs. The list below describes a variety of AT devices discussed by specialists such as Marshall Raskind and Kristin Stanberry (2015).

- *Abbreviation expanders:* These are software programs students can use to create, store, and reuse abbreviations for frequently used words or phrases. This can save the student with dysgraphia or poor spelling keystrokes and ensure proper spelling of words and phrases he or she has coded as abbreviations.

- *Audio books and publications:* Recorded books allow users to listen to textbooks and literature in a variety of formats. Special playback devices allow users to search and bookmark pages and chapters. Some highlight words or sentences as the voice moves across the text. Subscription services offer extensive electronic library collections in natural and synthetic voices. Certification of disability is needed for some subscriptions, but others, such as Audible.com, are available to all students.

- *Electronic math work sheets:* Using speech recognition technology, electronic math work sheets, such as MathTalk, allow students to dictate what they want to write as well as call up lengthy equations. This may be helpful for students who have difficulty with memory retrieval, numeric facilities, handwriting (dysgraphia), developmental motor coordination or who are reluctant to write everything out due to other cognitive processing nuances.

- *Graphic organizers and outlining:* Programs such as Inspiration, Kidspiration, and DraftBuilder support the writing process (from brainstorming through final drafts) while allowing for keyboarding and organization of ideas through both cluster maps and linear outlines. Writing is perhaps the most complicated of basic skills for individuals with learning differences to master, since it includes not only attention to details such as punctuation and grammar but also flexibility with language and following linear systems of thought development.

- *Behavior prompts:* Devices such as Watchminder and Motivater are visual and vibrating prompts that help students to independently stay on task, to remember to take medication, to think before acting, and a variety of other executive functions.

- *Personal FM listening systems:* Frequency modulation systems were originally developed for the hard of hearing. Their use, however, has expanded to a broader population (including individuals with attention deficits) in order to help them block out extraneous stimuli and stay focused in movie theaters, lecture halls, classrooms, and auditoriums. Individuals with auditory processing disorders and mild hearing loss may benefit from more accurate processing of auditory information using an FM system.

- *Portable word processors and notepads:* Word processors with and without keyboards can provide a whole host of support for students and are often the springboard for the kinds of media and technology espoused by the CCSS. Not only do they support executive function, organizational, and writing systems, they are critical to postsecondary success in personal, academic, and professional realms.
- *Speech-recognition programs:* Programs such as Dragon Naturally Speaking are appropriate for students who have difficulty with word retrieval difficulties, handwriting (dysgraphia), or developmental motor coordination or who are reluctant to write everything out due to other cognitive processing nuances. It's important to recognize that speech recognition systems are most effective for students with learning differences once they have been taught how to brainstorm ideas and develop an outline. From the outline, students can stay focused on the idea in order to dictate into the program.
- *Screen readers and speech output devices:* Originally developed for individuals with visual impairments or blindness, these applications allow individuals with a variety of learning differences to hear words that are on the screen. When encapsulated into writing-software programs such as Write Out Loud, students can hear the words they type immediately in order to provide real-time feedback for editing, clarity, proofreading, and self-monitoring. Other programs (such as Read, Write, Gold) offer screen reading, writing support, and highlighting in one system. Additional devices that support a vast array of learning differences include talking calculators, spell-checkers, and dictionaries.
- *Word-prediction programs:* Programs such as Co:Writer predict what words a student may want to use next in a sentence and generate a series of appropriate word choices. Not only does this remove the need for students to write long phrases such as *the Declaration of Independence* or *the Social Security Act* over and over, it ameliorates difficulty with word retrieval and word choice.

Accommodations

Accommodations can be aspects of instruction and tests. Some of the most comprehensive work done on accommodations within the classroom and on tests has been done since 1990 through the University of Minnesota at the National Center on Educational Outcomes (NCEO). The framework developed at NCEO groups test accommodations into the following categories:

- Presentation (repeat directions, read aloud, large print, braille)
- Equipment and material (calculator, amplification equipment, manipulatives)
- Response (mark answers in book, scribe records response, point)
- Setting (study carrel, student's home, separate room)
- Timing/Scheduling (extended time, frequent breaks)

These accommodations should be considered within the context of a student's needs and the limitations associated with those needs. Not all students need test accommodations, but when there is a match between a student's needs and the right accommodation, the student acquires an improved ability to demonstrate what is known or can be performed on assessments.

Instructional accommodations can be grouped in the same manner as test accommodations. The main difference is that instructional accommodations are designed to promote and facilitate the learning process rather than facilitate demonstration of knowledge or skills. Therefore, instructional accommodations include additional practice to attain mastery, additional scaffolding and teacher cues (that will eventually be removed), advanced organizers for upcoming reading assignments, a preview of advanced vocabulary in textbook chapters, work with the teacher to plan out long-term assignments, and the option to receive electronic prompts to stay on track as well as many others. Both test and instructional accommodations should be considered when evaluating how to address a student's particular need.

Accommodations on exams are critical for students who genuinely need them because we have not yet validated large-scale standardized tests with the principles of UDL. Therefore, it is imperative that teachers understand that the test accommodations indicated in a student's IEP or 504 plan become historical evidence that the student indeed needed the accommodation as a result of a specified learning difference. For example, school psychologists and teachers should be able to state why a student needs extended time or a distraction-reduced environment as it relates to his or her learning difference. Moreover, what evidence is there to support the connection? It may be teacher observation, test data, or informal data, but there should be some rationale for the recommendation in order for the student to take the test in as valid a format as possible.

Collaboration

When children are in elementary school, they typically have one or two teachers, which simplifies the process for collaboration between teachers, specialists, and parents. Even in elementary school, however, specific efforts must be made to inform all stakeholders in a child's education about what strategies, techniques, and ideas are being implemented in each classroom. In inclusive classrooms, general education and special education teachers need to collaborate in all phases of the teaching and learning processes. Bridging the resource room to the general classroom and vice versa is critical. In this manner, special education teachers can see their educational ideas and supports move into the general education classroom, and the general education classroom teacher can receive support from the learning specialist in the resource room. Even when a student is not in a special education program, the same collaboration should occur between private tutors or specialists and the general education teacher.

Few interventions work in a vacuum. Collaboration is the main vehicle to promote generalization of ideas across tasks and settings. In order for students to employ the strategies or techniques, practice across settings must occur. This is known as *generalization*. It starts when teachers explain all the techniques being used to one another and to guardians/parents. When a compensatory strategy is taught in a resource room, as part of an IEP, or as part of a general education classroom, every teacher should be taught to prompt that strategy use. If there are specialized teaching techniques, all teachers should be encouraged to apply these techniques. Students can be held accountable for where and how they have applied strategies. As a student moves into secondary settings, the need to collaborate becomes paramount, because there are many more teachers involved in the child's education.

Counseling and Self-Awareness of Strengths

The final aspect of the MASSive approach is perhaps the most difficult to acquire at school because it is psychological in nature. For some students, years of academic struggle have persisted to the point that the biggest obstacle to effective instruction is resistance and motivation. Despite the best approaches, a student may resist instruction for a variety of reasons, including depression, anxiety, mood disorders, or physical conditions. Even when teachers have attempted to motivate students through materials that are personally engaging and methods that are in line with the student's learning profile, some students will refuse to engage. In these instances, teachers should seek support from a school psychologist, appropriate school counselor, or other staff to provide mental health support. Moreover, consultation with the school or district behavior specialist can be a powerful tool in learning how to manage student engagement through behavior management systems.

As we have written, self-awareness of learning differences, effective strategies, and one's strengths and gifts are some of the biggest factors in promoting resilience for students with learning differences. Too often the emphasis is on what needs to be fixed or what is wrong. Teachers must consider how their daily interaction can promote self-awareness in order to prepare children effectively for life after high school.

THREE EXAMPLES OF THE MASSive APPROACH

The MASSive approach is unique because it helps teachers to target one need and identify a comprehensive approach that (a) promotes independent learning, (b) maintains commitment to the improvement of basic skills, and, (c) prepares students for postsecondary settings through the consideration of technology and accommodations.

Word Identification

Goal: Increase Word Identification Performance

- Compensatory Strategy: University of Kansas Word Identification Strategy
- Skill Building: Virtual Reading Coach by Mindplay (http://www.mindplay.com)
- Accommodation: Prompts on desks from all teachers to use Word Identification Strategy
- AT: Books on CD to be used with strategy
- Collaboration: Communicate with teachers in general education
- Counseling and Self-Awareness of Strengths: Develop a personal vocabulary list that includes words related to personal interests (trains, dinosaurs, engine parts, music, etc.). Use these words in word study activities.

Reading Comprehension

Goal: Increase Reading Comprehension

- Compensatory Strategy: University of Kansas Reading Comprehension Strategy
- Skill Building: Reciprocal teaching
- Accommodation: Different color Post-it notes to mark themes, characters, or other key ideas
- AT: Create concept maps with Inspiration software

- Collaboration: Get information ahead of time from English teacher to activate background knowledge through videos or online abbreviated notes
- Counseling and Self-Awareness of Strengths: Develop a personal reading list that includes materials related to personal strengths and interests

Written Expression

Goal: Improve Writing Fluency

- Compensatory Strategy: Graphic organizer with clear placeholders for key sentences
- Skill Building: Transition Words List
- Accommodation: Word processor and Transitions Words List
- AT: Use of mapping software such as Inspiration
- Collaboration: Support Transitions Word List across teachers
- Counseling and Self-Awareness of Strengths: Regularly work with student on writing that emphasizes personal pursuits: inventions, passions, amazing life dreams. Help student to see that he or she has ideas worth communicating!

THE MOST CRITICAL VARIABLE: PRAISE, PRAISE, PRAISE

Struggling learners come in a variety of forms. Many have difficulty with attention, impulsivity, distractibility, executive functions, and language or numerical processing. Some students have emotional issues or are in personal crisis or are exposed to detrimental environmental conditions. Some get all *A*s with an inordinate amount of effort, perseverance, and tears. Others get a range of grades with the same level of angst. Some want to do better and simply do not have the tools, support, or skills. These children often feel like something's wrong with them. All struggling learners despair about their performance in school and how they compare to their peers as well as meeting their parents' and teachers' expectations. They are especially sensitive to negative feedback when they think they've done a good job after great effort.

One aspect of an effective classroom management system is praise. Another aspect to working with students with learning differences who are resistant to instruction is to help them to become aware of how they learn. Most individuals like to know more about themselves and how to excel. Self-awareness of learning and dialogue can open doors for resistant students. It shows empathy, teaches empowerment, and creates self-understanding.

Teacher feedback has an enormous impact on student effort and willingness to persevere. Despite years of teacher education and research that underscores the importance of positive behavioral support, negative teacher feedback to students is rampant in schools. As consultants to a wide variety of schools and teacher educators in Northern California and Maryland, we see countless examples of teacher feedback on student work that is 100% negative with not one comment about what the student did correctly.

Nicole's Story

The work samples provided below show work by a seventh-grade girl with dyslexia, dysgraphia, and ADHD-combined type. This assignment took her twice as long as her peers. When I worked with her mother, she noted that the young girl worked slowly because she wanted desperately for her writing to be readable and to get at least a *B+*. With knowledge of the nature of this child's learning differences, the teacher could have praised many qualities in both samples of work, but she did not. The teacher, Ms. L, could have commented on the student's legible handwriting, good sentence structure, excellent artwork, following the majority of directions correctly (she did not return the Thematic Learning Unit cover sheet), turning in the work in on time, and other positive qualities. Instead, in both the writing and the math homework, only negative feedback was provided.

By her eighth-grade year, this student had such intense anxiety about learning and teacher criticism, she became terrified to interact with Ms. P, her new teacher, especially in math. This teacher had a reputation for being unapproachable and highly critical of students with learning differences. By the year's end, the student was getting *A*s on math homework and test corrections with her tutor and *C*s through *F*s on math tests in the classroom. Ms. P then determined the student had attitude problems, since she would not ask Ms. P for help. Ms. P did nothing to support the student's learning differences other than give her extended test time; she believed the student's real problem was her unwillingness to ask for help, pay attention, and follow directions. The student received a *D-* in math her final grading period despite her good work with her private tutor. Ms. P wrote poor references for this student's high school applications. At the end of eighth grade, she felt a huge sense of relief to be leaving the current school. When this student was tested for high school math placement at a rigorous college prep high school, she was placed into the advanced math class to be taken with sophomores. On the nationally standardized high school entrance test, she placed in the 75th percentile in math compared to her peers on national rankings. Ms. P's assessment of this student and discrimination regarding her learning differences was not isolated to this student yet she was subsequently promoted to a leadership role in the school.

Despite Ms. P's expectations, the student is now thriving at a college prep high school with an outstanding learning support specialist who teaches self-awareness, self-advocacy, and learning strategies. She asks for help and feels positively supported. All students, and students with learning differences in particular, need to know what they have done correctly as well as what needs to be improved upon or corrected. Parents can benefit from this awareness of praise. Teachers can be key individuals to mentor parents toward an environment of positive support.

(Continued)

(Continued)

No Til
-2
not double spaced
-2
No novel
-5
11/20

Along time ago there lived a wizard. Every morning the wizard would put on his light blue robe and elegant silver and blue hat and walk out to help teach people and guide with his wisdom. One day while the wizard was walking through the small town, he saw a little boy arguing with his parents.

"No mother it looks boring!"
The boy protested, stomping his foot and crossing his little arms. His mother sighed and handed the book to her husband.
"This book may seem boring but it is very fun and can teach you many marvelous things. Please at least give it a try"
The boy shook his head and began to walk away from his parents.
"Little boy"
The wizard called out. The boy's head turned, his eyes in marvel at the sight of the wonderful wizard. The wizard bent down so that his eyes met the boys.
"Oh my dear child, let me help you see why your parents are right. Meet me tomorrow at the top of the highest hill. My dear friend will be there to help me teach you"
The boy, cautious at first, agreed to go with the wizard to the top of the hill. As the wizard left the town he met with his dear friend, a lizard who he had known for a very long time.
"Lizard, you must help me teach my dear friend a lesson. Let me put a spell on you. You will have the ability to change color whenever you will like"
The wizard boasted about the great times the lizard will have with this wonderful new way of living. The lizard was unsure at first but after great persistence from the wizard the lizard agreed. The wizard jumped happily and took a vial from his pocket.
"Drink this lizard and then you will have this wonderful ability"
The lizard swallowed the contents of the vial, feeling no effect at first. Then the wizard stepped back and watched as the lizard changed it's color to the ground it was standing upon.
"It worked! It worked!"
The lizard cheered and jumped around as the wizard thought up his way of helping the boy.
"You are now a chameleon. That's the name of the special lizards who have this power"
The next day, the lizard and the wizard met the boy at the top of the tall hill.
"Are you hungry?"
The wizard asked the little boy. The boy, tired from the walk up the hill nodded eagerly.
"Pick an apple from that tree. Don't forget to pick wisely"

The boy walked towards the apple tree and studied the apples for minutes. The boy picked the most clean, shiny, and beautiful apple of them all. The wizard smiled and motioned for the boy to eat it. The boy bit into the apple but seconds later threw it to the ground and watched as the lizard fell off the apple, it's color changing from the bright red to the color of the ground it now stood on.

"That lizard was on my apple!! I swear it was not there!! It looked-"

"Like it was just the right one?"

The wizard cut him off, smirking. The boy sighed and rolled his eyes.

"You thought the apple looked perfectly fine, you bit into it and there was a chameleon in it. You saw that book your parents gave you, if you read it maybe it would have been a very good book"

The wizard picked up the chameleon only to have it crawl out of it's hands.

"You never said anything about being ate!"

The chameleon proclaimed, angered by the wizard. The boy nodded and walked back to town where he picked up the book and began reading it. A week later, the boy was walking through the forest by his town. He walked past a tree, at the sight of the boy the chameleon changed it's color. From the day on the hill on, chameleons change their colors to protect themselves.

(Continued)

(Continued)

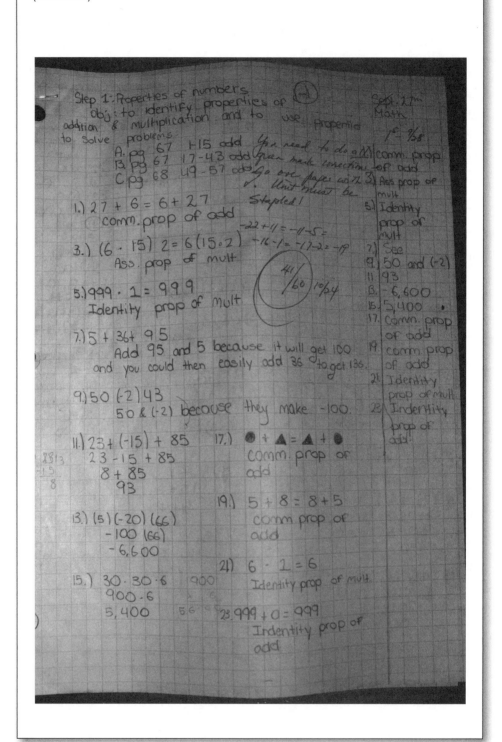

Many children who come under the lens of a formal educational evaluation do so in order to get help with interpersonal or academic needs. These needs often loom large in the minds of children and parents and sometimes cast attention away from what the child is doing well. When we pay attention to what children do appropriately, it not only gives them the attention all children crave but it also helps to balance out the challenging parts of their home and school lives.

How can parents and teachers work with children to support what they do well and appropriately? When a child (or any of us!) is rewarded for behavior, it increases. This works for both positive and negative behaviors. By far, one of the most common functions of all behavior in children is to gain attention. Telling children to sit down gives them just what they need: attention (though it is negative attention) or a way out of the activity. Every behavior has a function for a child. Many times, students will get a stomachache, produce inappropriate drawings, or have a tantrum at the beginning of math class (or other specific lesson). These behaviors may serve a variety of functions: power/control, protection/escape, attention, and so on. School personnel will often ask a behavior specialist to identify the function of a behavior when it is detrimental and frequent. Fortunately, most children seek attention through good manners, appropriate class behavior, academic achievement, creative hobbies, athletics, and other desirable behaviors.

The bottom line: We all want attention and will seek it out one way or another. As teachers of students and parents, we can use this knowledge about behavior to create positive and respectful relationships with the children in our lives and improve school performance. Moreover, praise increases the desire to be successful at other behaviors we teach at home, on the field, and in the auditorium.

We should pay greater attention to and not take for granted the simple behaviors our children demonstrate. Praising children for everyday tasks that are done well (or simply done) at home or at school can pave the way for children to feel secure in their environment. When children see teachers and parents paying attention to them and the little things they do, the ability to nurture new academic or personal behaviors is dramatically increased. Stop for a moment and ask yourself what behaviors you can praise in a student in your class. For some, the behaviors can be as basic as remembering to zip his or her backpack up so that nothing falls out, putting his or her name at the top of a page, hanging up his or her coat in the classroom, writing the homework down in his or her planner (even if it wasn't done or turned in!), making an attempt to organize a report, refraining from gossip with other students, asking for help, or getting out the door to get to school on time.

Nicole's Story

I once worked with a student who didn't come to school every day and who was quite abrasive to other students and teachers. Some teachers said, "What could we possibly praise this kid for?" We started with, "Thanks for coming to school today. It's good to see you." Any time he seemed to find a kind word to say to someone else, his teachers would quietly say something like, "That was a very kind thing to say; I'm sure it will be remembered." We even asked the school custodian to pay attention to the simple behaviors that allowed for the opportunity for praise. This paved the road, albeit a several-month-long road, for building the kind of trust and engagement we needed in order to work on academic goals.

Praise for small behaviors can lead to more significant behaviors. Many children do not necessarily know how one right step connects to another. Older students with learning and interpersonal needs often benefit from getting feedback on behavioral interactions, such as "I appreciate that you noticed I needed help just now with that heavy equipment. Thank you; it was very thoughtful" or "It's great that you turned your homework in today. I noticed it was not here yesterday. Thank you for remembering. I want you to do well!"

As you think about what kinds of behaviors you can praise and would like to see more of, it's good to keep in mind the arsenal of words at your reach. Too often we get in a rut of saying "Nice job." But varying praise can keep it new and, again, direct a child's attention to what's important. The list below provides a variety of words and phrases to keep your expressions engaging.

Words of Praise

Unbelievable work!

Phenomenal!

You've outdone yourself!

Your help really counts!

You are being very responsible.

Nothing can stop you now!

What a great example for others you are!

Look at what you made happen!

Breathtaking!

I can tell you listened carefully.

Incredible effort!

You're catching on!

I see you care.	Exceptional performance.
I knew you could do it!	Outstanding!
I'm so proud of you and you should be proud, too!	Nice going!
	You're amazing!
Looking good! You're so extraordinary at this!	You've made incredible progress!
Beautiful work!	Very thoughtful!
Now you're flying!	Congratulations!
Neat!	You really stuck with it!

By now you might be thinking this is all simply a combination of good manners and normal expectations for all children and perhaps wonder why we need to praise what is already in place. However, students with learning differences need to know what they did correctly as well as what needs improvement. Without this, school becomes a place of constant correction and defeat. Individuals who are strong learners receive praise consistently in the form of strong grades, no red marks on their papers, and many smiley faces! One way to accentuate the positive for students is to remember that all children need to believe that they are one of the best at something. They might be the classroom's best homework collector or board cleaner, the most spirited, or the most cooperative. As you wonder what you can praise and who is best at what, you may want to try the exercise out on a fellow teacher. Even grown-ups like to know they are still worthy of that gold foil star for an everyday kind of task.

Building a better classroom requires a change of perception and attitude and a willingness to learn and embrace new approaches in working with students with learning differences. It requires constantly helping students to note what they can do well, even if it's not part of their grade. By providing a nurturing environment and improving basic skills in our students, we will help them become better prepared to enter adulthood.

6 The Common Core: Teaching for a Lifetime or Teaching for One Way of Life?

The Standards define what all students are expected to know and be able to do, not how teachers should teach. For instance, the use of play with young children is not specified by the Standards, but it is welcome as a valuable activity in its own right and as a way to help students meet the expectations in this document.

—Core State Standards Initiative, 2014

Perhaps the most pressing challenge facing educators is the implementation of the Common Core State Standards (CCSS). The CCSS Initiative describes the CCSS as providing

a consistent, clear understanding of what students are expected to learn, so teachers and parents know what they need to do to help them. The standards are designed to be robust and relevant to the real world, reflecting the knowledge and skills that our young people need for success in college and careers. (CCSS, 2012)

The CCSS will drive curriculum and instruction for the foreseeable future. Implications are both positive and negative for students with learning differences and their parents. Understanding the wide range of possibilities leads to more effective advocacy and the ability to negotiate when necessary. Teachers and parents will better position themselves and their students through an analysis of this educational reform.

GOOD INTENTIONS, CHANGE, AND CONFUSION

Few would argue with the goals of the CCSS or the importance of clear and consistent expectations. We want education to prepare students for the real world. We also expect students to have mastered similar sets of knowledge and skills, thereby having a more accurate sense of what their high school diplomas represent.

In addition, the CCSS are aligned with an emerging sense of the skills needed in jobs, careers, and entrance into postsecondary education. According to a recent survey of the Association of American Colleges and Universities, 93% of organizations have concluded that a student's ability to "demonstrate a capacity to think critically, communicate clearly and solve complex problems is more important than [a candidate's] undergraduate major" (Hart Research Associates, 2013, p. 1).

As with all educational reforms, both positive and negative outcomes are possible. On the positive side, we will have a more valid rubric for comparing the performance of students from across the country. The anticipated result should effect greater educational equity from state-to-state and even district-to-district. With teacher evaluations closely linked to student performance, we will make teachers more accountable for their students' outcomes. In many visions of the reform, teachers whose students are not succeeding at expected levels will receive professional development and mentoring to make them more effective.

The curriculum framework of the CCSS is designed to add greater depth than current state curriculum standards. Students will develop better problem-solving and decision-making skills that are more applicable to the demands of the adult world beyond school. Students will be asked to broaden their conceptual understanding and rely less on rote procedures. Kris, a teacher who has skillfully integrated the CCSS into her class practices, shares that students

> are no longer taught the traditional algorithm for adding and subtracting—you remember, the regroup, carry the one, or 'borrowing' from the neighbor. Students now break numbers apart in their head to do the math (e.g., $42 + 38$ is thought of as $40 + 30 = 70$; $2 + 8 = 10$; $70 + 10 = 80$). It allows students a deeper understanding of what is truly going on in the problem while simultaneously creating greater number sense. . . . I have seen a

HUGE growth in children who have been exposed to the CCSS and its new approach to learning. Students who are just finishing second grade have been exposed to it now for three years. Overall, we have a much lower number of students entering third grade 'below grade level.' This is truly amazing!

As much as new curricular and instructional approaches hold promise, transition and change are rarely without cost. The same teacher voices her concern on how the CCSS are communicated to parents and students:

As for the parents, they are struggling with it, too. They certainly aren't used to learning the way we are now teaching—and students who are receiving assistance from parents for homework are coming back to school more confused than when they left for the day. Parents are confused as well.

According to policy makers, the CCSS will offer greater support and more professional development. Thus the system offers hope to students who simply are not receiving the instruction they deserve. However, teachers who work with larger populations of at-risk students may be summarily blamed for mandated outcomes that do not necessarily take into account the individual challenges these students face. It remains unclear whether the CCSS will help students with learning differences to make greater gains under its implementation. In this section, we review what we believe to be positive characteristics of the CCSS, what we term *the Good*. That which may or may not make much of a difference to students with learning differences we refer to as *the Meh*. That which we have serious concerns about we refer to as *the Bad*.

THE GOOD

Two of what we believe to be *the Good* aspects of the CCSS are the major underpinnings of Universal Design for Learning (UDL) and assistive technology. For over twenty years, the paradigm of UDL has gained momentum in the field of education. Both special educators and general educators alike have embraced the notion that education can be designed so that it is accessible to all students. The main question has always been how to make it accessible for everyone. The Center for Applied Special Technology (http://www.CAST.org) set out to explicitly show teachers how to help students with and without disabilities to diversify the learning experience through resources, technology, teaching methods, and engagement. Their model is practical and guided by neuroscience. While the UDL paradigm incorporates a significant amount of technology in order to foster a wide range of educational options, this paradigm does not rest solely on technology per se. One reason why UDL works so well within the CCSS, however, is because the CCSS place a heavy emphasis on technology; therefore both concepts, UDL and technology, can work in concert in order to allow students with learning differences to access instruction and demonstrate knowledge. A third aspect of *The Good* is that the authors of the CCSS clearly state the limitations of the framework and standards. We review what the CCSS are not and discuss other aspects of the CCSS Initiative that we believe all teachers need to know and understand in order to lead students with learning differences to be successful with the standards.

Universal Design for Learning

A concise definition of UDL was provided by the Higher Education Opportunity Act of 2008 (HEOA), which stated

> The term Universal Design for Learning means a scientifically valid framework for guiding educational practice that:
>
> (A) provides flexibility in the ways information is presented, in the ways students respond or demonstrate knowledge and skills, and in the ways students are engaged; and
>
> (B) reduces barriers in instruction, provides appropriate accommodations, supports, and challenges, and maintains high achievement expectations for all students, including students with disabilities and students who are limited English proficient.

UDL is a powerful methodology because it allows teachers to diversify instruction while maintaining clear goals and objectives for each standard or lesson. In fact, teachers start with clearly articulated goals and objectives for teaching and then diversify. The diversity of instruction goes beyond what teachers know as differentiated instruction. Teachers consider how instruction can be modified for each students and the diverse ways the knowledge can be demonstrated for each student.

Based on neuroscience, the UDL paradigm shows teachers how to (a) present content and information in different ways (Representation), (b) differentiate the ways in which students can express what they know (Action and Expression), and (c) stimulate interest and motivation for learning (Engagement). (See Figure 6.1 for more details.) Representation of content includes consideration of perception, language, expression and

I. Provide Multiple Means of Representation

1: Provide options for perception
1.1 Offer ways of customizing the display of information
1.2 Offer alternatives for auditory information
1.3 Offer alternatives for visual information

2: Provide options for language, mathematical expressions, and symbols
2.1 Clarify vocabulary and symbols
2.2 Clarify syntax and structure
2.3 Support decoding of text, mathematical notation, and symbols
2.4 Promote understanding across languages
2.5 Illustrate through multiple media

3: Provide options for comprehension
3.1 Activate or supply background knowledge
3.2. Highlight patterns, critical features, big ideas, and relationships
3.3 Guide information processing, visualization, and manipulation
3.4 Maximize transfer and generalization

Resourceful, knowledgeable learners

II. Provide Multiple Means of Action and Expression

4: Provide options for physical action
4.1 Vary the methods for response and navigation
4.2 Optimize access to tools and assistive technologies

5: Provide options for expression and communication
5.1 Use multiple media for communication
5.2 Use multiple tools for construction and composition
5.3 Build fluencies with graduated levels of support for practice and performance

6: Provide options for executive functions
6.1 Guide appropriate goal-setting
6.2 Support planning and strategy development
6.3 Facilitate managing information and resources
6.4 Enhance capacity for monitoring progress

Strategic, goal-directed learners

III. Provide Multiple Means of Engagement

7: Provide options for recruiting interest
7.1 Optimize individual choice and autonomy
7.2 Optimize relevance, value, and authenticity
7.3 Minimize threats and distractions

8: Provide options for sustaining effort and persistence
8.1 Heighten salience of goals and objectives
8.2 Vary demands and resources to optimize challenge
8.3 Foster collaboration and community
8.4 Increase mastery-oriented feedback

9: Provide options for self-regulation
9.1 Promote expectations and beliefs that optimize motivation
9.2 Facilitate personal coping skills and strategies
9.3 Develop self-assessment and reflection

Purposeful, motivated learners

Source: © 2011 by CAST. All rights reserved. www.cast.org, www.udlcenter.org APA Citation: CAST (2011). *Universal design for learning guidelines version 2.0.* Wakefield, MA: Author.

symbols, and comprehension. The demonstration of knowledge includes physical action, expression and communication, and executive function. Engagement includes recruiting interest, sustaining effort and persistence, and self-regulation. Examples and resources for implementing UDL can be found online (http://CAST.org) and in Figure 6.1.

How is this different from what we have come to know as *differentiated instruction*? Essentially, UDL provides a blueprint for not only considering the individual needs of the learner, but it allows for the individualization of materials using technology (e.g., text to speech, speech to text, recording devices, prepared notes), instruction (e.g., closed captioned, video, immediate feedback), and assessment (e.g., oral presentation, written presentation, artwork).

One simple example comes from a sixth-grade classroom in Palo Alto, California, where students were required to select one piece of historical nonfiction from a booklist. Students were allowed to access the text through reading, text enlargement, text to speech, and video to accompany the text. Students were then given three ways of demonstrating their knowledge of the book. First, the teacher made clear that the goal for the assessment was for each student to show an understanding of the main characters, the plot, and their opinion of the book, stated in professional language. The three options included creating a one- to two-minute video, writing a book review, or designing and creating a book jacket. Thus students who are technically and visually inclined would have the option to capitalize on their strengths via the video option. Students who are highly verbal would likely select the book review, and students with nonverbal strengths could choose the book jacket project.

In addition to individualizing the method of assessment, students were able to use a variety of materials to compensate for individual strengths and needs. One student with dysgraphia selected the book review and dictated her story via a speech-to-text system. Another student with dyslexia listened to his text through an audiobook while he followed along, then he created a video. The Center for Applied Special Technology website offers a wealth of materials to help teachers understand the different modalities individuals use to recognize and encode information, assimilate it, and demonstrate knowledge. Throughout the process, learners come to appreciate their own strengths and talents. This in and of itself is a significant contribution to the ongoing healthy development of the self and resilience.

Emphasis on Technology

The CCSS also emphasize the widespread use of technology. For example, students in middle and high school are required to use the Internet to produce, edit, revise, and publish writing. Technology is significantly incorporated in the math standards through, for example, the use of calculators, spreadsheets, protractors, graphing, and statistical programs and to display data. As seen in the discussion above on UDL, technologies—specifically Assistive Technology—can be important vehicles not only for delivering instruction via Smart Boards, instructional software, and presentation software but also for offering students multiple means of working with text. If the CCSS are designed to prepare students for work and postsecondary education, technology is unquestionably a critical component.

Shelley Pasnik, director of the Center for Education and Technology, calls technology *double innovation* because teachers must first learn how to use it and then determine if and how it fits into the goals and objectives of the classroom (Cleaver, 2014). When done effectively and with school-based tech support, technology is a powerful method to level the playing field across socioeconomic levels, languages, and learning differences. Once students have access to the Internet, they are no longer constrained by limited resources for books, libraries, and information. As we discuss later in this chapter, however, the stark reality is that some school districts still do not have the financial resources to support technology in the classroom.

Why is technology vital to the success of all students and those with learning differences in the era of the CCSS? Technology in the general sense brings to mind computers, word processing devices, electronic notepads, calculators, Smart Board technology, and an array of software. These forms of technology are critical components of the CCSS because they easily work alongside or function as ways to ameliorate many limitations associated with learning differences. Students with learning differences can minimize error and maximize the fluent application of knowledge. While technology is not a replacement for teaching nor does it make a learning challenge go away, many devices can indeed compensate for functional limitations associated with a learning difference or disability. This is more important than ever, since the CCSS explicitly call for instruction in reading and writing that is embedded in application rather than as a separate learning activity. If individuals have specialized needs for reading and writing instruction and there is a greater emphasis on inclusion, teachers must be able to use technology as a compensatory strategy for students who are not reading and writing at grade level. Moreover, some low-tech devices are not even hardwired; they are typical resources or educational supplies found in almost any classroom. Below is a sampling of low- and high-tech devices to support students with learning differences.

Individuals with fine motor challenges or dysgraphia may benefit from

- A keyboard instead of a pencil or pen
- A slant board (a slant board resembles a closed 3-inch binder)
- Speech-to-text systems
- Assorted writing devices designed to fit different finger grips
- Large square graph paper to line up and organize math problems
- Recording pens (such as Livescribe)
- Electronic applications that facilitate annotation (such as Notability)
- Word processors with alphabetic keyboard as opposed to QWERTY keyboard
- Brainstorming software (such as Inspiration or MindManager)
- Colored Post-it tabs to follow actions among characters, plot, or themes

Individuals with reading challenges or dyslexia may benefit from

- Text-to-speech systems
- Audiobooks
- iPad applications that allow for annotating while reading and electronic highlighting
- Changeable background and foreground colors when reading
- Computer screen magnifiers
- Keyboard with reversals distinguished
- Colored Post-it tabs to follow actions among characters, plot, or themes

Individuals with inattention and distractibility may benefit from

- Noise-cancelling headphones
- FM systems to reduce distractibility and increase focus on the spoken word
- Visual-spatial timers (desktop or as an app) such as TimeTimer (http://timetimer.com)

For all students, use of Smart Boards allows teachers to provide students with copies of lectures via video or electronic notes in order to facilitate comprehension and to review material after class and before subsequent classes. Closed captioning on videos allows all students the opportunity to follow along through reading as well as listening, and for some students, this genuinely aids language comprehension. Therefore, teachers should consider captioning before using videos in class. Technology has the potential to reduce the impact of learning differences and strengthen access to the CCSS curriculum when implemented with thoughtful consideration.

Perhaps one of the biggest challenges related to the implementation of the CCSS is the use of technology to represent multiple ways to teach a concept or lesson. It is here that we often observe a difference in teacher preparation programs as they relate to technology and assistive technology. Many general education teachers become proficient at using technology as an instructional method or as a vehicle for delivering instruction but are not familiar with AT. Conversely, special education teachers become familiar with AT, but many are not proficient at the use of general forms of technology as an instructional method or resource tool. As teachers become more familiar with UDL and how that influences the transition of instruction into AT, we can begin to use technology to its fullest capacity.

Let's look at an example. A unit on oppression, prejudice, and racism may include literature such as *Heart of Darkness,* a textbook chapter on the economic and political factors that influenced the slave trade around the globe, a class lecture guided by presentation software such as PowerPoint or Prezi on the civil rights movement in the United States, a video that can be viewed at home, and an online learning module with only PowerPoints and recorded voice. Technology clearly plays a huge role in this unit. The richness of bringing a variety of materials and methods to teach a subject has inherent appeal to both teachers and students.

How can teachers accentuate this technology in order to make it accessible to all learners and especially those with learning differences? Let's start with the assigned literature and textbook. Are they offered in electronic text so that students have the option to listen to the text? Does the teacher provide an outline of the lecture presentation so that students can take notes without recopying information on the slides? Does the teacher provide a video recording of the lecture so that it can be replayed at a later date? Is the at-home video close captioned? The online module could be developed to be captioned and amenable to a screen reader. Therefore, when we embrace technology as an aspect of the CCSS, we must remain cognizant of UDL and AT. Only then can we genuinely make the most of the most recent advances in technology for all learners.

Explicit Recognition of What the Standards Are Not

The CCSS include up front what they are not. Unfortunately, this is a small part of a large document that contains some powerful information. We say *unfortunately* because what is contained in this section of the CCSS are the caveats that give teachers the freedom to engage students in a myriad of creative and meaningful ways. This flexibility allows all learners to succeed. Perhaps because the CCSS were ushered in with an aura of significant change and controversy, many regard them as rigid and fixed. Yet this section of the CCSS clearly encourages play, which would include theatre and art, freedom of content, diversity in instruction, and advanced curriculum.

The notion that standards-driven education can allow for academic freedom is crucial for all teachers. Teachers bring their own unique skill sets to the classroom, many of which include Socratic dialogue, theatre, media arts, puppetry, music, art, humor, and the ability to meet students face-to-face in ways other teachers cannot. These methods can still be incorporated in a standards-driven education. Furthermore, teachers are given the freedom to modify text in order to meet the needs of their learners. Teachers still have the autonomy to select a variety of texts that motivate and engage students based on their interests. We encourage teachers to be more creative than ever before in this era of standards-driven education. Standards provide a uniform expectation so that all children can reach adulthood successfully. The notes in the box below encourage teachers to bring their best skills to the classroom in order to help students attain that success.

What Is Not Covered by the Standards

The Standards should be recognized for what they are not as well as what they are. The most important intentional design limitations are as follows:

1. The Standards define what all students are expected to know and be able to do, not how teachers should teach. For instance, the use of play with young children is not specified by the Standards, but it is welcome as a valuable activity in its own right and as a way to help students meet the expectations in this document. Furthermore, while the Standards make references to some particular forms of content, including mythology, foundational U.S. documents, and Shakespeare, they do not—indeed, cannot—enumerate all or even most of the content that students should learn. The Standards must therefore be complemented by a well-developed, content-rich curriculum consistent with the expectations laid out in this document.

2. While the Standards focus on what is most essential, they do not describe all that can or should be taught. A great deal is left to the discretion of teachers and curriculum developers. The aim of the Standards is to articulate the fundamentals, not to set out an exhaustive list or a set of restrictions that limits what can be taught beyond what is specified herein.

3. The Standards do not define the nature of advanced work for students who meet the Standards prior to the end of high school. For those students, advanced work in such areas as literature, composition, language, and journalism should be available. This work should provide the next logical step up from the college and career

readiness baseline established here. The Standards set grade-specific standards but do not define the intervention methods or materials necessary to support students who are well below or well above grade-level expectations. No set of grade-specific standards fully reflects the great variety in abilities, needs, learning rates, and achievement levels of students in any given classroom. However, the Standards do provide clear signposts along the way to the goal of college and career readiness for all students.

4. It is beyond the scope of the Standards to define the full range of supports appropriate for English language learners and for students with special needs. At the same time, all students must have the opportunity to learn and meet the same high standards if they are to access the knowledge and skills necessary in their post-high school lives.

5. Each grade will include students who are still acquiring English. For those students, it is possible to meet the standards in reading, writing, speaking, and listening without displaying native-like control of conventions and vocabulary. The Standards should also be read as allowing for the widest possible range of students to participate fully from the outset and as permitting appropriate accommodations to ensure maximum participation of students with special education needs. For example, for students with visual disabilities, *reading* should allow for the use of Braille, screen-reader technology, or other assistive devices, while *writing* should include the use of a scribe, computer, or speech-to-text technology. In a similar vein, *speaking* and *listening* should be interpreted broadly to include sign language.

6. While education language arts (ELA) and content area literacy components described herein are critical to college and career readiness, they do not define the whole of such readiness. Students require a wide-ranging, rigorous academic preparation and, particularly in the early grades, attention to such matters as social, emotional, and physical development and approaches to learning. Similarly, the Standards define literacy expectations in history/social studies, science, and technical subjects, but literacy standards in other areas, such as mathematics and health education, modeled on those in this document, are strongly encouraged to facilitate a comprehensive, schoolwide literacy program.

Source: Authors: National Governors Association Center for Best Practices, Council of Chief State School Officers. (2010). *Common Core State Standards: What is not covered by the standards.* Washington, DC: Author.

THE MEH

Urban Dictionary defines the *meh* as "indifference" (Lauder, 2002). It is hard to ignore some of the redundant, unoriginal, and unnecessary qualities of the CCSS that many teachers, policy makers, and parents may be indifferent about.

Education Driven by Standards

Not much is new about education mandated and governed by federal standards. Beginning with Goals 200 and then No Child Left Behind, to many, the CCSS are more of the same old standards-driven education. While the educational philosophies behind the CCSS are quite different than previous standards movements, they are still federally driven. Regardless of the ongoing controversy of the early 1990s centering around states' rights to their own standards based on local needs versus federal standards based on the needs of a country, public education is being fueled by the CCSS. Most politicians and educators agree that we need a general framework with which to articulate what we expect all students to know and be able to do. General controversy persists about what those expectations should be. Should we be preparing *all* students for college? A large body of individuals would like to see the design arts and trade skills returned to high schools. This is now largely in the hands of technical, vocational, and two-year colleges. CCSS advocates argue that high school students will be prepared to enter these types of programs with adequate preparation. Nevertheless, many still believe that high school graduates should be given the opportunity to enter the workforce directly from high school without undue pressure to move on to college. At eighteen years of age (that is, young adulthood), they should have the autonomy to decide what comes next.

In spite of good intentions, the CCSS may not bode well for students with learning differences. While they do not dictate a curriculum, they contain a framework for curriculum design that dictates what students should learn and defines successful academic preparation as college readiness. It dramatically narrows the content taught by focusing solely on college and career readiness in a limited manner. As a result, it will make it terribly difficult for teachers to address adult issues or life skills for individuals who, for legitimate reasons, are not on a college or career path. The CCSS insist on mastery without considering multiple pathways to life after high school and the difficulty of the curriculum for students with learning differences. Instead, we should be developing creative new approaches that capitalize on the strengths of students with learning differences.

Large-Scale Assessments to Monitor Standards

As was true with the standards-driven education movement, we are still in an era of accountability. Assessment of the CCSS is very new, and some states are still piloting the assessments at the time of this writing. The Partnership for the Assessment of Readiness for College and Careers

(PARCC) is made up of approximately thirteen states that collaborate on the development of assessments of the CCSS and is just one avenue of assessment. The PARCC assessments are both paper and computer-based in math and English/language arts/literacy. Some students such as those in Westerly, Rhode Island, participate in a practice lab twice a week in order to prepare them to take tests online. For both the paper-based and computer-based tests, a large number of test accommodations are available to meet the needs of students with disabilities. These, however, are not available for all students. The assessments are worth knowing about by teachers because the test design incorporates features of universally designed assessments and technology.

For example, PARCC has designed the paper-based tests with accessibility features for all students. The computer-based tests have comparable accessibility features. A student can use external highlighters, place markers, masking devices, colored overlays, different writing instruments, or pointers. These same features are built into the computer-based version.

California and New York were the first two states to pilot assessments. The first round of scores for students in New York suggested poor performance on the CCSS. This is not necessarily bad news. CCSS assessments will need to be refined in order to determine whether they indeed match what is being taught in the class; pilot testing should allow test developers to reevaluate the alignment of the test content with the standards. Moreover, it will take several years for teachers to fully understand how to adopt and implement the CCSS. Large-scale tests are designed, in part, to show how schools are doing in implementing the CCSS. While public outcry may see it solely as how students and teachers are doing as a whole, these large-scale tests also provide important information to the federal government about how resources such as technology and professional development should be allocated in order to improve school performance.

Nevertheless, the emphasis on testing worries many teachers. Students with learning differences tend to have special difficulties on standardized formal tests. The No Child Left Behind Act's reliance on standardized testing, often referred to as *high-stakes testing*, exacerbated inequities faced by students in special education. The pressure increases with the CCSS. The bottom line on the CCSS is that students have to pass end-of-year state assessments. Performance will determine whether they are promoted and ultimately graduate. In addition, teachers will be evaluated by how their students perform on CCSS testing. Promotion, tenure, and job security will depend, in part, on student performance on assessments.

Consequently, students with learning differences find themselves in classrooms where the focus on teaching becomes improving test scores. One of the chief concerns among teachers today is being held personally accountable for all diploma-bound students passing challenging standardized tests. The pressure intensifies for teachers working with students with learning differences. Teachers who are anxious and harried produce students who are anxious and harried.

Peter Attwood, a senior systems software engineer contributing to a special education discussion group on *Linked In*, puts it bluntly:

> Common Core is more testing kids to death, actual learning be damned. It and all the rest of the project to reduce education to test-taking and standardized testing, while turning kids into a profit center for edbiz, is a disaster for all kids.

Paradoxically, we highly recommend teaching test-taking skills. Many students with learning differences can present themselves more positively and more accurately with improved test-taking skills. But this is only a small part of education and, really, an artifact of using tests that do not necessarily do a good job of measuring critical skills. In our ideal world, we would not have to teach students how to take tests. Instead, we would directly assess their behaviors and aptitudes in order to provide the most useful formative and summative feedback.

The CCSS express a reaction to the shocking decline of U.S. education in international rankings. Although a legitimate concern, these rankings need to be understood within context. Most countries do not reach out to the diversity of students as the American system does. The United States educational system is a free and public education that provides basic education to all children in the country. To an extent, we compare our students to what are essentially elite groups of students from other countries. Even countries such as the United Kingdom that offer a free and public education to all children still test students to determine if they are university-seeking or vocation-seeking at an early age (about our equivalent of high school). In most cases, results from other countries do not include those of students in special education. The American educational reforms that respond to these rankings literally do not take the needs of students with learning differences into account. We hope to raise our national scores on assessments used by other countries with different populations, different needs, and different views of social justice and educational equity. Let us hope this process does not result in further marginalization of students with learning differences.

THE UGLY

Cognitive Demands of CCSS and Students With Learning Differences

Few educators pause to reflect on what new methods of instruction require from a student in terms of brain functioning and cognitive demands. More often, the consideration is on content, recall, and application of learning. We know much about the mind, brain, and education, but how often do we consider what is required in terms of information processing and executive functioning when we plan a lesson? The researchers at the Center for Applied Special Technology, through the UDL paradigm, have contributed a wealth of information and training to teachers in this area. Other prominent neuroscience researchers such as Albert Galaburda, Gordon Sherman, Kurt Fischer, Jane Holmes Bernstein, Mary Helen Immordino-Yang, and Lynn Meltzer have contributed major breakthroughs about the brain and learning as well. How does cognitive functioning relate to the CCSS?

> ### Nicole's story
>
> As an educational specialist, I work with students across the grade span in schools where the CCSS are being implemented by well-trained teachers. As I watch the CCSS being incorporated into today's classrooms, I see unprecedented demands being placed on two main areas of cognition: flexibility with cognition and making connections between a large number of materials and media. These qualities are valuable in the education of our children. Consequently, teachers will need to be aware of them in order to better communicate lessons and learning.

Cognitive Flexibility

Deák (2003) writes,

> Flexible cognition entails the dynamic activation and modification of cognitive processes in response to changing task demands, representations and responses based on information. As task demands and context factors (e.g., instructions) change, the cognitive system can adapt by shifting attention, selecting information to guide and select upcoming processes, forming plans, and generating new activation states to feed back into the system (e.g., goals, self-correction). If these processes result in representations and actions that are well adapted to the altered task and context, the agent can be considered flexible. (p. 275)

Cognitive flexibility is one aspect of executive functioning and a characteristic weakness of many individuals with different types of learning differences. Because the CCSS emphasize synthesizing multiple forms of text and resources as well as multiple representations of content, students are required more than ever before to shift their cognition rapidly and to understand which information is relevant. This is an important skill for students to learn and master because this is a key aspect of college and work. On a daily basis, students are required to sort through the tasks at hand, prioritize, follow directions, and determine what the best approach to the tasks should be. These tasks can include taking notes during a lecture, extracting relevant information from different texts, relating this information in different ways (e.g., short answers, multiple-choice questions, or essays), applying math concepts in words and calculations, and so on. Cognitive flexibility has always been an aspect of learning, but the CCSS framework emphasizes the need to change one's thinking quickly and effectively in all areas of learning.

Teachers can help students shift their thinking by teaching them how to use and apply learning strategies such as goal setting and self-monitoring. Similar to using a car's GPS, teachers should think about their final destination in a lesson plan and how they are going to take students there. This road map should be communicated to students along with critical markers so that they know when they are astray from the end goal. These critical markers can take the form of a checklist or rubric, self-questioning strategies, and peer review.

Making Connections

The CCSS have set an unprecedented level for students' use of critical thinking. They do this in a variety of ways. One way that poses a challenge to students with learning differences is the huge amount of connections students must make among materials and resources. Because the CCSS aim to foster familiarity with different types of text and resources for all subjects, it is not unusual for one topic to be taught with many types of materials. However, students with learning differences and many struggling students do not readily make connections between the materials and the topic. In our experience, teachers tend to provide a variety of information-rich materials (e.g., textbooks, primary source readings, literature, research articles, or video), but students are left to distill what is pertinent to the topic. It is only when the materials are literally mapped out by listing them on a sheet of paper or drawing them on a board and then asking students to talk about the main idea of each one and then how that relates to the topic that they are able to make the important connections. More often, students tend to read or peruse each resource as a separate entity in and of itself with the belief they need to understand the entire document.

Without explicit instruction in how materials are connected, students with learning differences do not relate them to the topic at hand or understand the interconnectedness. Teachers cannot assume that our students are making these connections on their own in the era of CCSS.

Lack of Resources for Professional Development and Technology

UDL and technology are, as we stated earlier, very good aspects of the CCSS. We believe that technology is inescapable in today's education. Schools that effectively implement technology hire personnel to not only maintain equipment but who can educate teachers on new devices and how to use them and who can stay abreast of technological advances. However, it takes money to fund technology and all that is needed to implement it successfully. Many schools still do not have resources to purchase books, let alone technology. Moreover, technology is not just about software, hardware, applications, devices, and platforms. Individuals must know how to use it in order to support curriculum standards and individual devices. This takes ongoing professional development and technical support. How will these schools succeed in implementing the richness embedded in the CCSS? To complicate issues for students with learning differences, poorer schools tend to have a higher prevalence of children with learning differences who also need assistive technology in order to succeed. We question whether the CCSS will provide equity for all students, at least in this arena.

7 Self-Understanding

In order to succeed, people need a sense of self-efficacy, to struggle to-gether with resilience to meet the inevitable obstacles and inequities of life.

—Albert Bandura

The foundation for satisfying adulthood is an intact sense of self. This chapter explores a number of approaches teachers and parents can use to empower their students to see themselves as whole and compe-tent. The process begins with an intentional effort to build positive interpersonal and intrapersonal relationships. The use of the Individual Education Program (IEP), psychoeducational evaluations, and informal assessments provide powerful tools to facilitate this process. The Indi-viduals with Disabilities Education Improvement Act (IDEA, 2004) strongly supports parental involvement. Parents should be equal par-ticipants in their students' educational decision making. Involvement of parents, especially within the school system, improves the process and leads to improved student performance.

> Almost 30 years of research and experience has demonstrated that the education of children with disabilities can be made more effec-tive by . . . strengthening the role and responsibility of parents and ensuring that families . . . have meaningful opportunities to par-ticipate in the education of their children at school and at home. (IDEA, 2004)

Working effectively with students with learning differences requires collaboration and a team approach involving not only parents, teachers, counselors, administrators, and other professionals but students them-selves. Students will have an easier time building a positive sense of self when they are part of a supportive team with a winning attitude. All part-ners in the team advocate for the best interests of the student. In many cases, the teacher plays the role of the primary facilitator and mediator.

BUILDING A SENSE OF SELF

The key to teaching for a lifetime is straightforward: Prepare your students with learning differences to be the best they can be. The goal is simple; the process is not, but it is neither mystifying nor overwhelming. People who have a strong self-concept, solid self-esteem, and confidence in their ability to take on challenges fare better in life than those who don't. Success in any endeavor requires resilience as well, another outgrowth of self-confidence. Specific strategies can build a positive sense of self that acts as the founda-tion for future success in all areas of adulthood.

Learning differences usually are detected because of academic failure. These are kids who are beaten down by the educational system. They are constantly reminded of their weaknesses with little attention given to their strengths. They often have difficulty with interpersonal relationships not-withstanding the amazing abilities of some students who excel and com-pensate through their social acumen. From what we understand, they are often hardwired in such a way that behaviors of executive function, particu-larly attention and deep processing, do not come naturally, compounding their risk for academic and social failure.

The world does not always make sense to them. We expect our intentions to help us adapt. The eminent psychologist Carl Rogers (1951, 1959, 1961), stressed that congruence of who we believe we are with the outcomes of how we act is critical in developing self-actualization. Children with learning dif-ferences start off believing in themselves, feeling they are positive and capa-ble individuals, as all children do. Early in life, our dreams are limitless, from being superheroes to having every toy in the world. Psychological develop-ment requires that we reframe, but for most of us, the reframing allows us to establish a sense of positive adaptation. We may not get every toy, but if we do what our parents tell us, we will get a toy. Our sense of self leads to actions that are rewarded and reinforce our sense of personal capability.

The message that students with learning differences often receive is that they are not capable. To continue the example, they try to please their parents, fail, and do not get a toy. They do not understand why they failed to please and are left wondering why their sense of who they are does not get positive outcomes. This lack of coherence leads to a disconnect from their selves and their relationship to their environment. They manifest this disconnect in many different ways. Some are clearly defeated; the only response that makes sense is to give up.

An elementary teacher observed a phenomenon that virtually all teachers have experienced:

> At our professional development meeting last month, we were talking about helpless hand raisers. Helpless hand raisers are those students who raise their hands for everything, including to ask questions you have already answered or just to raise their hands.

Some students are incredibly impulsive and can't seem to help themselves. They may not be exercising executive function to monitor their behavior. Others take on a different persona that gives them a more satisfying explanation of their place in the world. They become troublemakers, class clowns, or victims. As Sally Smith, founder of the Lab School in Washington DC, has written, they wear masks to hide their learning differences.

When teachers are not willing to reframe their own thinking about students who learn differently, these kids question their deepest sense of self-worth. The majority of students with learning differences whom the authors have advised and counseled have had great difficulty answering the question, "What are your strengths?" On the other hand, they are quick to list their weaknesses. Students who have a negatively skewed self-image invariably have relationship trust issues. Why should they trust people who chronically put them down and make them feel they are a failure? When this is the overall experience of going to school, a student with learning differences may be reluctant to trust any teacher, even a teacher who tries to reach out and help. These students are often suspicious for good reason. In their experiences, interactions with teachers have only gone in one direction. At the end of the day (literally), many, many kids with learning differences feel bad about themselves.

Successful adults with learning differences use positive self-attributes to build mutually satisfying relationships. Academic success is a building block that begins with teachers and parents helping students to discover and capitalize on their strengths while acknowledging and creating action plans to compensate for weaknesses. Teachers, parents, and counselors also have important roles in helping students understand and utilize their emotional intelligence. All the while, development of executive functions will provide students with the basis for managing both academic and social/emotional demands.

Students routinely acquire and utilize proactive academic and behavioral skills. The Princeton Review, Kaplan, and other test-preparation agencies guarantee higher scores on the SAT. These programs do not make kids smarter. Rather, these students learn, practice, and implement effective test-taking skills. We can teach students how to manage time, be better organized, plan, and prioritize for both cognitive and social/emotional demands. Students with learning differences are capable of building a repertoire of skills. These learning strategies help them with academic demands as well as functional challenges in the adult world.

Internalized attributes underlie behaviors. These, too, can be learned. Positive experiences teach students to have more confidence and a better sense of self. Specific activities help adolescents and young adults understand their strengths and weaknesses. Counseling, both formal and informal, encourages self-reflection and a more honest appraisal of who one really is. Students can learn to build better interpersonal relationships. They can learn how their emotional selves should work for rather than against them.

IMPLICATIONS FOR ADULTHOOD

Children who feel bad about themselves grow up to become adults who feel bad about themselves. Feelings of inferiority, inadequacy, weakness, helplessness, and dismay evolve as dysfunctional behaviors. Adults who lack a sense of self-worth question the value of effort, ambition, and their ability to form meaningful and satisfying relationships. They have learned to be helpless as adults and use their learning differences as a reason or excuse not to try. Conversely, children who feel good about themselves are more likely to turn into adults with a positive view of the world and their place in it.

One of the roots of successful adult outcomes is supportive parents and teachers. Parents are most likely to be aware of and in touch with their children's feelings. They see the sense of defeat their kids bring home. Successful adults with learning differences routinely remember that a parent—most often but not exclusively their mother—was the person who understood what they were going through. At the end of horrific days at school, they would tell their mother how awful they were feeling. Parents provide great assurance simply by listening. Some parents take an even more active listening role, reassuring their children that they are okay, complete individuals. They rewrite the messages being sent by the educational experience. They explain that the disconnect is not the fault of the child but rather a lack of understanding on the part of teachers or other students. They help the child create a better sense of coherence about the school experience.

A relatively simple approach—positive affirmations—adds to this process. We tend to overlook moments for positive affirmations, especially if we constrain ourselves to the normal boundaries of school achievement. Opportunities abound to "catch 'em being good," from picking up their room to surviving a difficult day. Some of us had mothers who would put a little note, a positive message for the day, in our lunchbox. Unconditional affirmation can push back the negative input that is so often a part of the school day.

Parenting a child with learning differences is difficult. Extraordinary determination, fortitude, and sacrifice go with the territory. One teacher recounts a particularly impressive mom who advocated for her child despite less-than-ideal circumstances:

> We had an IEP meeting for this student yesterday. I have to say I am truly impressed with the mom. She has come to realize the severity of the issue and told her work that she'd need to cut back her hours to be home for her son when he got home from school. They said that wasn't possible and they'd have to let her go. She said okay. When her job saw she was serious, they did allow her to cut back her hours. I was so very proud of mom for standing up to her employer and putting her son first! I thought that was huge, especially since this child speaks very poorly of his mother and her boyfriend. He certainly isn't nice to her, and I would think that would make it even more difficult to want to be around him more. Kudos to mom!

Yet many parents do not know what to do, especially to make things better. They try to listen, but they are not able to understand the disconnect. In spite of good intentions, they reinforce the negative messaging that the child hears at school. Their child struggles for no apparent reason. Perhaps the child does not try hard enough. Maybe something is wrong with their child.

When children internalize that sense of inadequacy, they exhibit a phenomenon known as *learned helplessness*. They do not see the point of trying when it only leads to failure. Now the parents' concerns are justified, at least in their own minds. They inadvertently add to the child's sense of being a loser. They show concern, often by expressing their frustration to teachers and administrators. They may seek tutoring or counseling in an effort to improve the situation. They are attempting to fix their child.

Think about how it feels to be told you need to be fixed. You really are incapable. Others are now controlling your very sense of self. People are doing things *to* you, not *with* you. Everyone is trying to help; you feel reduced to a broken and helpless being.

Not to Toot My Own Horn

Keely, guidance counselor

First, I was someone who had a learning disability. I am not ashamed, as I have come to understand that I learn differently from my peers. However, as someone who had an IEP, I can understand the process, the labeling that society places upon students and the stigma that has always been held over my head ever since I was tested. Since I have hearing loss in both ears, it was difficult to grasp speech as I should have. (I have now, but not when I was younger.) This created issues with my reading development and my speech. My special education teachers were always special to me. They never judged me, and they taught me as if nothing was ever wrong. In my experience in the special education classroom, I met several individuals with learning disabilities, several students who had dyslexia, and more and more students with ADD [attention deficit disorder]. As I went through school, I learned to adjust to my disability by working hard and asking questions. Overall, I believe I will always have some form of disability, but I have conquered how to learn my way.

My disability never got me down. I just had to work twice as hard as my peers.

Throughout elementary school, a few of my teachers sent me for testing because they suspected I had ADD. I remember getting yelled at in second grade while my teacher was reading a story because I was looking at the floor and she thought I wasn't paying attention. But I was, I was just imagining in my head what she was reading. I also could scarcely read or write at that point, and I remember that she used to get very frustrated with me because I would make light of what I was struggling with. I used to be quite the class clown, believe it or not. After being tested by professionals a few times (with no diagnosis of ADD), she began working with me after school. She came to understand me as a person and how I learned and, long story short, by the time I was taking state tests, I was scoring in the upper 95th percentile every time (for English, at least). Not to toot my own horn.

Another reality faced by some children with learning differences is systemic family dysfunction. Not all parents are nurturing. For whatever reason, they choose not to be supportive or may lack the capacity to do so. Blame becomes the predominant dynamic. Emotional and physical abuse is certainly not limited to children with learning differences, but the outcomes may be even more pernicious. It is almost impossible to be resilient if the whole world, starting with the parents, is undermining the very essence of who the child is. In this sense, some children with learning differences really are broken. Maybe a fix is in order, but it needs to be holistic and focus on the environments that have brought on this despair as well as the child. Human beings can heal. The role of the support team is to begin the healing process.

SKILLS FOR BUILDING RELATIONSHIPS

Kids don't learn from people they don't like.

—Rita Pierson

Students who fail invariably have strained relationships, beginning with themselves and extending to those around them. Low self-worth leads to avoiding challenges (i.e., learned helplessness). Many students with learning differences will be defensive and guarded, no matter how open we think we are. If left unchecked, learned helplessness can undermine adult autonomy. A case worker described one of her clients with exactly this type of condition:

> This individual was in his early thirties. He would make comments like, "I'm too hyperactive to work," and "My ADHD [attention deficit/hyperactivity disorder] prevents me from staying focused at a job." I worked with him for about a year, and every time I would volunteer to job hunt with him, I would get turned down. I even told him I would pose as a friend and not his case manager if it was the stigma of a mental health worker helping him find a job that was deterring him from accepting my help. He still turned it down. Towards the end of my time working with him, he got social security income which, in my opinion, made him even more complacent with hanging out with friends all day. I know he had a rough childhood because his birth mother was on welfare and put him in the foster care system. This probably is a case of history repeating itself, but I refuse to let a person's history define their limitations on what they can do in life. I have this expectation for everyone, not just him.

It may be that this young man was already conditioned to look for excuses, and ADHD was convenient. It is also much more difficult than most of us realize to break this cycle. A child with learning differences may grow up with needing to have excuses; at least excuses are not total admissions of failure. Excuses become the norm. Dysfunctional behavior from childhood becomes dysfunctional behavior in adulthood.

In the adult world, making excuses simply does not work. Businesses want workers to do their jobs correctly. To say that a task did not get done because of one's ADHD does not cut it. Incompetence is not protected under the Americans with Disabilities Act (ADA). Making excuses never gets anybody anywhere.

Children who feel good about themselves are more likely to show responsibility and accountability. The more one is secure, the less one is defensive. The secure person does not blame the world when things go wrong but rather tries to find a way to make things better. How do we help our students build the confidence and resilience to not make excuses or resort to learned helplessness?

Positive and constructive relationships are nonjudgmental, an elusive process in a school environment that centers on judging students through never-ending assessments. To borrow from the philosophy of Rogers, we build the strongest relationships through unconditional positive regard. In counseling married couples, Rogers extended this to unconditional love.

Saul McLeod (2007) concisely articulated this concept:

> Unconditional positive regard is where parents, significant others (and the humanist therapist) accept and love the person for what he or she is. Positive regard is not withdrawn if the person does something wrong or makes a mistake. The consequences of unconditional positive regard are that the person feels free to try things out and make mistakes, even though this may lead to getting it worse at times. People who are able to self-actualize are more likely to have received unconditional positive regard from others, especially their parents in childhood.

What a great recommendation for teachers! Making the worthwhile effort to build a one-to-one relationship with students with learning differences begins with a realization that they have, at best, received a great deal of *conditional* positive self-regard. At the far end of the spectrum, they have experienced mostly unconditional negative regard. They have learned to see themselves as less than whole. They need to learn new ways of looking at themselves. Even more challenging is the process of unlearning the negativity and leaving the damaged baggage behind.

The daughter of one of the authors was fortunate to attend a small private school. Although it was not geared toward students with learning differences, the small class size and attention to individual needs largely compensated for a lack of specialized teaching approaches. The mission of the school was an intentional effort to make every student feel valued. When students walked into the building at the beginning of the school day, the director was standing at the main entrance. He hugged every single child who entered the school. We do not know if this public display of affection would be acceptable in a public school. Too bad. It was the most important moment of the day. It set a tone. The students knew they were walking into a setting where they were loved and affirmed just for being themselves. Think about the impact this gesture would have on all the children who doubt themselves and the people around them.

Teachers are in a great position to offer this type of encouragement. Any successful educational intervention starts with building a relationship of trust and security. A great way to start to build a positive relationship is to let students know that they matter. Angela Maiers (2014) recommends that teachers try the 2-5-2 method on a daily basis:

- [Greet your students] by name as they enter the class, and then make a positive remark about several students in the first **two** minutes of class.
- Commend at least **five** students in each class period for their contributions to the discussion.
- Finally, reserve **two** minutes at the end of each class to reflect on what everyone learned that day.

Value your students. Demand they be the best they can be. Show them that you are willing to be a champion for them.

As we have seen, models of success tout the importance of being a good listener. The best thing we can do for our students is to listen to them. Good teaching starts with assessment and observation—which include listening—to discover the best approaches to teaching and learning. We feel valued when we know someone is actively listening to us. Maybe your favorite teacher was the one who took the time to listen to you.

We have adapted suggestions from Adrienne Jones (2013) for parents who do not have children with disabilities to support parents who do. These approaches are also helpful tips for anyone trying to build positive relationships with students with learning differences:

- Listen. Just listen. Open yourself up. It can be uncomfortable and scary to acknowledge that a child is in pain. Don't leave him or her alone with it.
- Know that you can't fix it. Don't try. Instead, talk about strengths while acknowledging the reality of weaknesses.
- Acknowledge and affirm. Say, "Wow that sounds hard." Say, "It must be very difficult for you."
- Treat kids with learning differences the same way you treat other children in your life. Engage kids in conversation. Say hello. Smile.
- Offer to help, but only if you mean it. Share that help is an ongoing process that ultimately puts ownership on the student.
- Spend time learning about the child's diagnosis.
- Keep listening. Just show up and listen. There's nothing any person in pain needs more.

SOCIAL SKILLS AND TEACHABLE MOMENTS

Social and behavioral skills are a better determinant of lifelong success than are academic skills. People who have highly effective social skills are more likely to be hired and retained than people who do not. Persons who lack social skills often make the workplace environment difficult for others. *Dealing with Difficult Employees* is one of the most common workshops in the business world. In many cases, the best solution is to fire them.

Paradoxically, social skills training receives scant attention in school. A student who does well academically but has poor social skills often does not pop up on the teacher's radar. A child who does not have many friends—well, that's just how it goes. Ignoring these types of situations may severely limit opportunities for a satisfying adulthood.

As a student becomes older, weak social skills may begin to have an effect on academic and functional performance. Knowing how to work with instructors and fellow students is often a critical element in performing well in high school, college, and postsecondary education. Being able to work in groups is becoming more and more of a prized skill, beginning in elementary school and extending to many careers. In many cases, poor social skills lead to lower self-confidence, beginning the insidious cycle of a defeatist attitude.

As any good teacher will tell you, the most valuable learning often occurs in unscripted moments. In the same way that we talk about living in the moment, we need to talk about teaching in the moment. Many of the areas that this book encourages teachers and parents to address—particularly social skills—are included only peripherally in most curricula and not at all in some.

Slowly, some schools are incorporating social skills into their curriculum and instruction. At one teacher's charter school,

> every day, as part of the curriculum, we have character education lessons. During this time, we teach students about the importance of respect and emotions as well as bullying issues and drugs. Teaching in an urban setting, my students are exposed to so many things at a young age that it is our responsibility to teach them right from wrong at times.

Sarah, another teacher, told us,

> This last week at school, I used a teachable moment to teach some of my students the importance of holding the door behind you. There are so many unwritten rules that need to be taught. We often take these for granted.

It is not only students with learning differences who benefit from social skills training in the moment. Another teacher in a general education class responded to Sarah:

It's interesting that you said you were teaching your students the importance of holding the door for the person behind you. This is something I focus on every single day. I purposely watch the students to see if they are using these skills. . . . It doesn't matter if our focus is teaching reading, math, writing, and social studies; we also need to focus on teaching social skills.

As we will see throughout this book, many of the concepts used to facilitate successful transitioning of students with learning differences to adulthood are equally applicable for all students.

Throughout the day, we are presented with opportunities to help our students acquire valuable skills, especially social skills. Most kids pick up on social skills by seeing how others act. They adopt behaviors that are socially appropriate and get positive results. Students with learning differences often do not pick up social skills through observation. As we have discussed, some social difficulties result from deficits in nonverbal language processing. On top of that, students who have weaknesses with executive function do not recognize relevant details and have difficulty processing cause-and-effect phenomena around them. They may not see a relation between, for example, holding a door and a pleasant response. They do not integrate the many unwritten rules of efficacious social interaction. As a result, they experience the incongruence between intention and the desired result, which may slowly wear down a positive sense of autonomy.

The following questions will help children and adults determine whether they need to work on interpersonal skills:

- Do I often say the wrong things at the wrong time?
- Do people shy away from me when I am just trying to be sociable?
- Do I have trouble understanding jokes?
- Do I feel overwhelmed in social situations?

The authors have worked with some extremely bright and capable college students with Asperger's syndrome who are so beset with anxiety (and are also impulsive) that they need constant reassurance and additional explanation. Their anxiety overrides their executive function. With one student who started dominating the class with constant questions, we agreed on a contract where he could only ask three questions per class, although he could follow up with the professor after class. It actually helped his anxiety to have defined structure. Equally important, he learned to behave in a socially appropriate manner.

THE IEP AS RELATIONSHIP BUILDER

All students are different. All relationships are different. And the circumstances for each relationship are different. Let's begin where the teachers have an invitation to build personal relationships with students with learning differences—students who have IEPs.

In our experience working with teachers in general education, most of them do little more than take a cursory glance at the IEPs of students diagnosed with special needs. They generally focus only on the accommodations they are required to make, rarely wanting to know why these accommodations are important. They deny themselves the opportunity to take advantage of the plethora of information the IEP provides.

Components of the IEP

The following information comes directly from the Center for Parent Information and Resources website (2010) and promotes a closer examination of the IEP:

The Big Picture

The IEP team broadly considers the child's involvement and participation in three main areas of school life:

- the general education curriculum,
- extracurricular activities, and
- nonacademic activities.

What an IEP Must Contain

The IDEA requires:

A statement of the child's **present levels of academic achievement and functional performance**, including how the child's disability affects his or her involvement and progress in the general education curriculum;

A statement of measurable **annual goals**, including academic and functional goals;

A description of how the **child's progress** toward meeting the annual goals will be measured, and when periodic progress reports will be provided;

A statement of the **special education and related services** and **supplementary aids and services** to be provided to the child, or on behalf of the child;

A statement of the **program modifications or supports for school personnel** that will be provided to enable the child to advance appropriately toward attaining the annual goals; to be involved in and make progress in the general education curriculum and to participate in extracurricular and other nonacademic activities; and to be educated and participate with other children with disabilities and nondisabled children;

An explanation of the **extent, if any, to which the child will not participate with non-disabled children** in the regular class and in extracurricular and nonacademic activities;

A statement of any **individual accommodations** that are necessary to measure the academic achievement and functional performance of the child on State and districtwide assessments;

(Note: If the IEP team determines that the child must take an alternate assessment instead of a particular regular State or districtwide assessment of student achievement, the IEP must include a statement of why the child cannot participate in the regular assessment and why the particular alternate assessment selected is appropriate for the child); and

The **projected date** for the beginning of the services and modifications, and the anticipated **frequency, location, and duration** of those services and modifications.

Extra IEP Content for Youth with Disabilities

The IEP must also include statements about what are called *transition services*, which are designed to help youth with disabilities prepare for life after high school.

IDEA requires that, beginning not later than the first IEP to be in effect when the child turns 16, or younger if determined appropriate by the IEP team, the IEP must include:

- measurable **postsecondary goals** based upon age-appropriate transition assessments related to training, education, employment, and, where appropriate, independent living skills; and
- the **transition services** (including courses of study) needed to assist the child in reaching those goals.

[For secondary students, the IEP addresses pertinent issues for preparing for life after school, the essential question we pose at the beginning of this book: What happens to children with learning differences when they grow up? No tool is more critical than a transition plan. A good transition plan represents years of work and planning. It provides the bridge to the first steps of adulthood.]

Also, beginning no later than one year before the child reaches the age of majority under State law, the IEP must include:

- a statement that the child has been informed of the child's rights under Part B of IDEA (if any) that will transfer to the child on reaching the **age of majority**.

A Closer Look at Each IEP Component

Present Levels: How is the child currently doing in school? How does the disability affect his or her performance in class? This type of information is captured in the "present levels" statement in the IEP.

Annual Goals: Once a child's needs are identified, the IEP team works to develop appropriate goals to address those needs. *Annual goals* describe what the child is expected to do or learn within a 12-month period.

(Continued)

(Continued)

Special Education: The IEP must contain a statement of the special education and related services and supplementary aids and services to be provided to the child, or on behalf of the child.

Supplementary Aids and Services: Supplementary aids and services are intended to improve children's access to learning and their participation across the spectrum of academic, extracurricular, and nonacademic activities and settings. The IEP team must determine what supplementary aids and services a child will need and specify them in the IEP.

Program Modifications for School Personnel: Also part of the IEP is identifying the program modifications or supports for school personnel that will be provided.

Extent of Nonparticipation: The IEP must also include an explanation of the extent, if any, to which the child will not participate with nondisabled children in the regular class and in other school settings and activities. [This mandate connects to IDEA's foundational principle of the least restrictive environment (LRE).]

Accommodations in Assessment: IDEA requires that students with disabilities take part in *state or districtwide assessments*. The IEP team must decide if the student needs accommodations in testing or another type of assessment entirely. In this component of the IEP, the team documents how the student will participate.

Service Delivery: When will the child begin to receive services? Where? How often? How long will a "session" last? [This is often the most valuable aspect of the IEP, since it gives parents and teachers a clear understanding of what will happen during the school day in order to meet the goals.]

Parents and students are an integral part of the IEP team. They need to feel engaged, empowered, and respected as a critical resource for developing the best plan. Unfortunately, in many cases, parents find themselves marginalized in the process. One teacher observed,

> Families felt they were not being listened to or supported in their ideas/beliefs during these IEP meetings. As one woman even described, "They come in with their own agenda and already know what they want; they don't ever give us a chance to talk about what we want." This particular woman wished for the school system to become more involved in her child's physical therapy. While she was unsure if this would be able to occur, she at least wanted the opportunity to have the conversation. That being said, while the IEP is incredibly important to make sure that everyone is on the same page with regard to a child with learning difference, it can often be a plan that is skewed towards the school's faculty.

Students with learning differences should have a more active role in the IEP process to facilitate buy-in and personal ownership. This transformation is unlikely to occur unless teachers and parents know how to navigate the

IEP process. When parents are unsure or are intimidated, teachers need to take on the additional role of educating and empowering parents.

A SYSTEMATIC APPROACH TO BUILDING SELF-AWARENESS, SELF-EFFICACY, AND AGENCY

Students who are familiar with their IEPs are more likely to have a sense of their strengths, weaknesses, and needs. They have a better understanding of goals and objectives. For students finishing high school, active participation is critical for making a successful transition to what lies beyond.

The psychoeducational evaluation is the basis for the IEP and offers a comprehensive overview of a student's strengths and weaknesses and overall learning style. A good evaluation explores the reasons for how a student learns. One approach that has been used for twenty years at a small college (McDaniel College located in Westminster, Maryland) is called Learning Disabilities: From the Inside Out and is designed to teach self-awareness of one's learning profile as represented in the individual's psychoeducational evaluation. The independent study is structured as a three-part project with guiding questions.

To begin the project of self-assessment, the students seek to understand the context for being identified with some type of learning difference. They ask their parents, if available, about the circumstances that led to concerns about educational performance. The student also tries to remember what was occurring at school and personally at the time. Although memories of childhood are often inaccurate about specific details, the feelings of how the individual perceived the experiences associated are real. Looking back on the events surrounding their entry into the special education or an alternative educational system, many adults with learning differences will refer to a sense of loss of control (Reiff, Gerber, & Ginsberg, 1997). Recollecting childhood experiences from a young adult vantage is empowering. In gaining an understanding of why the often-mysterious and threatening testing process occurred, the student is able to assimilate a more nuanced perspective and mitigate the negative associations of this experience.

The guided questions for the independent study encourage students to concentrate on strengths. The limited information that most students access about their evaluations tends to point out the reasons that they have been diagnosed with disabilities and the implications for special education services. Whether intentional or not, the messages resound of weaknesses and often result in negative self-perceptions. In few cases do students walk away from the testing experience with an enhanced self-image. Most have not read their own diagnostic evaluations.

As a result, many students with learning differences, even those who have been successful enough to matriculate at the college level, do not have a clear sense of their academic and personal strengths and cannot articulate them. The process of reviewing the psychoeducational evaluation with a trained professional allows students, sometimes for the first time, to see their strengths identified by an expert and credible source. The process redefines positive attributes in a way that is deeper and more transformative than words of encouragement from parents and teachers. Often, the experience of *disability* is reframed with a greater understanding of both strengths and weaknesses. The following projects were completed by Michelle, a college student with learning differences. The study requires completing three projects. Each project is described below:

Project 1: The student reviews all pertinent evaluations and assessments related to his or her learning differences. Based on careful and thorough analysis, the student will write a five-page (or more, if needed) paper synthesizing this information. The paper should be free of technical terminology; instead, it represents an attempt by the student to express his or her understanding of the learning differences. In a sense, the paper should be a portrait of the student, a narrative synthesizing various psychoeducational evaluations. As much as possible, the description should be understandable to someone not familiar with learning differences. The following questions serve as guidelines for Project 1:

1. What do you remember (if anything) going on before you went for an evaluation (e.g., poor grades; difficulties in school or home; retained in a grade; tutoring; anxiety, frustration, confusion, etc.)? Had this been going on for a while? How old were you?

2. Interview your parents about this period in your life. Why did they have you evaluated? What were their specific issues? Did the school/teacher suggest it? Why?

3. What do you remember about meeting with the person who did the evaluation? What kind of tests did you do (not the names of the tests you took but the types of things you actually had to do)? How did you feel—scared, didn't care, pleased?

4. What do you remember about what happened after the evaluation came back? Did you talk about it? Did anything change at school (e.g., did you wind up in a special class)? Did anything change at home?

5. Now look at the evaluation report with a staff member from disability support services. What tests (names) were given? What were the results (scores on tests and subtests)? What do they mean? What were the conclusions and recommendations in the report?

6. Do you agree with this report? Why or why not? What are your strengths? Be broad. Be creative. Talk to people who know you well.

At the time of the self-study, Michelle was a second-semester freshman at a small private liberal arts college in the mid-Atlantic region. Based on the psychoeducational evaluation report, she entered the college with a diagnosis of ADHD and was receiving support services. The entire narrative she wrote for the independent study is not provided due to length. The abbreviated interpretation of test results, however, unflinchingly identifies relative weaknesses. She devotes more attention to discussing strengths, in many instances as ways to compensate for weaknesses.

MY INTERPRETATION OF TEST RESULTS

I. Intellectual Aptitude

- The main test for intellectual aptitude was the Wechsler Adult Intellectual Scale.
- My performance IQ, which I interpret to mean how I do academically, was average, but my verbal comprehension was somewhat better than average. My ability to retain what I hear immediately in class is on the lower end of the scale, but when I am learning about something that I understand, I learn it quickly—and better than other people learn it (which may explain why I know more about alpacas than many people who have been in the business for years, but struggle with classroom issues that some people get much faster).

II. Verbal Abilities

The main tests for verbal ability were the WAIS-III and Woodcock-Johnson-III.

- I identify words and letters pretty well but have more difficulty on an auditory level, where it is hard to single out meaningful information against distractions. The tests also raised the issue of my selective attention, which I interpret to mean that when I understand or am interested in a subject, I can process the information better than when the subject is either too difficult for me to understand or I am not interested in the subject.

(Continued)

(Continued)

- *My verbal fluency was very good and I was able to retrieve information relevant to the topic of discussion very quickly.*
- *My listening comprehension was generally in the average range, which did not surprise me. One of the things I find to be the most difficult is to be talked at. I just don't learn this way and the tests showed that I struggle with directions and that I become frustrated while listening to directions.*
- *My oral expression skills were below average, which surprised me until I understood that this did not mean my capacity to express myself speaking but rather my capacity to recall things orally that I saw in a book.*
- *My vocabulary development scores were very high, and I have always felt good about my ability to learn words. It was interesting to see that the tests showed that I have trouble applying my knowledge to practical situations, which may explain some of the difficulty I had in social situations, especially when I was younger.*

III. *Nonverbal Processing*

- *There were a number of tests in the nonverbal processing category, including several in the WAIS-III and Woodcock-Johnson-III subcategories. I found it difficult to understand what each of these tests showed but understood better what some of them meant on a practical level.*
- *My ability to read nonverbal cues was rather weak, which may also explain some of my social difficulties years ago.*
- *My capacity to recall geometric and other figures was extremely poor. I apparently don't differentiate well between shapes and more complex figures. I thought this might help explain why I don't learn well by being talked at or in classroom environments, because in that type of learning, I am being asked to remember something that has no meaning to me. In other words, I don't know why I'm being asked to learn this.*
- *I was happy to see that I tested well at tasks that required coordination, processing speed, and creativity. I interpreted this to mean a few things. When I work with alpacas, I am able to identify them quickly and individually faster than other people. I can memorize their genetic lineages in great detail. I can even imitate their facial expressions and personalities, which I also learn very rapidly. With animals, I understand why I need to be able to differentiate between them because it affects their well-being.*

IV. *Attention and Executive Functioning*

- *The rating scales for attention and executive functioning included the Conners-3 Rating Scale, which took into consideration input from my parents and teachers and myself. In addition, the Delis-Kaplan tests were used.*

- *Unsurprisingly, there was strong consensus that I struggle with attention, focus, and anxiety. I interpreted the fact that I rated well above the clinical cut-off for attention-related issues to mean that there is little argument on my issues of attention, focus, and anxiety.*
- *These challenges also cross over into my social life—or, at least, they did during the time period when these tests were administered.*
- *The theme of my struggles with auditory working memory confirm why what I think of as classroom learning isn't the most efficient way for me to process information. Maybe auditory working memory is a more scientific way of saying I don't learn well by being talked at.*
- *There were a few contradictory conclusions about my ability to shift between activities. On certain tests, I struggled with going from one task to another, which is consistent with attention-deficit and focus challenges. On other tests, I did well sorting objects into different categories. When I read this, I thought of how successful I am with differentiating between the genetic lines of alpacas, which relates to being able to categorize complicated objects.*
- *My organizational skills were lacking, especially in what I consider to be my ability to juggle and prioritize tasks. This may help explain why I become overwhelmed when I have a lot of academic assignments; it's often hard for me to know where to begin.*
- *Consistent with my self-evaluation, the testing showed a disparity between my ability to read and write and my ability to make sense of math and science. This may point me in the direction of a major and career where I can exercise my above-average abilities to communicate through writing (and orally) and avoid math and science.*

Michelle's analysis of results from the Wechsler Adult Intellectual Scale and Woodcock-Johnson Tests of Cognitive Ability III demonstrates an ability not only to connect the results with experiences in the classroom but also to assert that she has the capacity to apply her strengths. She has worked on an alpaca farm for a number of years and has helped with the management. Her view of *selective attention* is not self-critical but rather an explanation of why she processes more effectively when she is interested. Her perception of her behaviors moves toward a more extrinsic or optimistic explanatory style (Kamen & Seligman, 1987). Although her information processing presents challenges, she is able to assimilate new materials, particularly when she can connect them to activities. She is not surprised by many of her verbal weaknesses. Instead of expressing frustration or a sense of defeat, she is able to understand the relationship between how she processes information and her academic challenges and advocates for herself by asserting that she does not like being talked at, a reaction that many of us may share. She establishes the congruence that Rogers describes as central to healthy self-autonomy. Her understanding of self when she states, "I struggle with directions and I become frustrated while listening to directions," corresponds to the outcomes of how she acts.

Michelle concedes that she had difficulty understanding the concept of nonverbal language but nevertheless applies it to everyday situations. She reflects on social difficulties as a child. Again, she raises the theme of being talked at and discovers another nuance for her behavior. The nonverbal strengths she gleans from the testing—"coordination, processing speed, and creativity"—please her and are compatible within her experience. She identifies her skills with alpacas and animals as a strength. In another part of her report, she concludes that she is more comfortable with animals than with people. Her analysis of the testing provides a sense of meaningfulness to this predilection and presages self-efficacy. The integration of self-understanding and one's relationship to the environment is another example of the concept of congruence.

The Conners-3 Rating Scale and Delis-Kaplan tests held little in surprise for Michelle. She came into the project with a high degree of awareness and acceptance of her ADHD. Her theme of not doing well with being talked at again arises. Certainly, issues of distractibility and anxiety can easily interfere with active listening. It is possible that her self-reported anxiety makes this situation circular: She does not do well when being directed, which raises her anxiety, which predisposes her to finding the situation aversive. As with other areas, she seems to accept relative weaknesses while concurrently focusing and applying her strengths. She demonstrates a capacity to use the results of the testing to explain her interests and goals and utilizes the information to assist with future decisions. This is a clear example of building agency and self-efficacy.

Project 2: Based on the analysis and synthesis from Project 1, the student will write a five-page (or more if needed) paper exploring how the characteristics and behaviors associated with the learning disabilities affected him or her in school, particularly at the university where the student is currently enrolled. The student should refer to specific examples. For example, if the paper from Project 1 described difficulties with being able to remember things that are said (i.e., auditory short-term memory), Project 2 might relate what it was like to take notes in a lecture and, perhaps, what the student did to compensate. The following questions serve as guidelines for the second paper.

1. Think about any classes where you've had real difficulty. Why? How much do you think could be related to your learning disabilities? How much to other reasons? Were you aware of these reasons at the time?

My whole life I have struggled with anxiety and ADHD, which makes school very challenging for me. Apart from these issues, I also get frustrated very easily because I find certain school concepts very difficult to grasp while other people seem to get them much more easily. I do much better in small classes, which is one of the reasons why I wanted to attend this college.

I still tend not to do very well in a conventional academic environment. I have concluded that I simply do not process information by being talked at; however, I have been able to develop expertise in areas where I am not forced to process information in this way (such as history or animal welfare). This has been confirmed by the academic and psychological testing I have had done over the years.

Teachers have rarely been able to explain things to me in a way that I understand. One of my math teachers, Mr. T, was the only one who would take his time to explain things until everyone understood perfectly, which frustrated most students. Because he was patient with me, I felt comfortable enough to ask questions until I fully grasped the subject. Teaching style is very important to me. If I sense that a teacher is annoyed with having to work with me, it triggers a cycle of resistance to learning that is impossible to break. I feel that a part of the reason I did not ask questions was due to my anxiety. I was anxious that my peers would not respect me if they knew how difficult it was for me to understand things that came so easily to them. My fellow classmates that struggled with math understood my challenges and, eventually, all of my classmates respected my issues and we even poked fun at my horrible math skills.

I had a different teacher who did not explain things as well; he just wrote on the board and expected us to understand, and if we didn't, he was unconcerned. This was another example of my not being able to learn by being talked at.

In my first semester of college, I did not perceive that my ADHD got in the way during classes. When I was not in class, however, I found it hard to focus on my study materials and I would get very easily distracted. With the freedom of college, it is much easier to be distracted and I realized this through trial and error. Hopefully, I will be more effective in addressing this going forward.

Michelle expresses the same themes as related in Project 1. Her lack of elaboration is not surprising, as she has used her experiences in school to provide a context for most of the psychoeducational findings. She does garner new insights about the effect of ADHD and learning differences in the college environment, where dealing with free time represents a considerable challenge.

2. In what classes have you used specific compensations and/or accommodations (e.g., special ways to study, talking to professor, extra help, extended time, etc.)? Were these approaches helpful? Why or why not?

> *The accommodations I received in middle school consisted of extra time to complete tests, usage of a calculator, and to be placed into a small group setting to take a test. At college, the disability services office gave these same accommodations plus note taking, where a student in my same class takes notes and I get these notes after a week or so. I never received notes from my history teacher because he never followed up after I gave him my note taking slip the first week of classes. I assume that I would have found my note taking accommodation very helpful, but I never received any notes. This may suggest some kind of disconnect between the teachers and academic support functions at the school, which would not be the first time I have encountered such challenges.*

Michelle is aware of accommodations she receives and needs. She does not make a clear connection between the learning characteristics described previously and the reason for the accommodations. She also demonstrates a need for more effective self-advocacy by her unwillingness to follow up with her history professor (understandably intimidating for a first-year student) or support services. Although she has the right to expect provision of accommodations, the reality of the demands in college require her to bring the disconnect to the attention of support services. She exhibits external loss of control in her failure to act and take ownership. Students with this perspective will benefit from a discussion with a learning specialist from support services.

3. In what classes have you been most successful? Why?

> *I loved my history classes in high school, mainly because my teacher would teach by laying down the facts and explaining what had happened. For example, he would tell you what happened in a certain war, including dates, names, and who won the battle.*
>
> *In my junior and senior year of high school, I had an excellent English teacher. We read good books, which were discussed throughout the entire class. The students would talk about their feelings and interpretations of the book. I rarely participated, mainly because the discussions would turn into abstract arguments and I preferred to observe others discussing the subject. I had difficulty in my science classes, once again due to a poor communication with my teacher, who found my disabilities very frustrating to deal with. She did not understand that scientific materials, especially labs, simply did not register with me.*
>
> *Sometimes the subject was not the main challenge, it was the teacher. I had math teachers who were able to explain things better than an English teacher, so I would do better in a class where, on an intellectual level, it was actually more difficult. In middle school, I did well in math because I had a wonderful teacher.*
>
> *At college, my most successful subject would have to be my first year seminar, Gender, Literature, and Culture. There was a lot of reading, which I did not like, but the papers were interesting. For my final paper, I had to write about gender roles in Disney films. I have a lot of knowledge about Disney movies and recalled them in great detail, so this was a fun topic for me.*

In this response, Michelle connects learning characteristics she has identified with her strengths and successes as a student. Similar to many students with ADHD, she responds more readily when material is clear, organized, and concrete. Her evaluation indicated difficulties with abstract reasoning; she accordingly sees the relation between this style and problems in classes where "discussions would turn into abstract arguments." Michelle's educational history indicates a weaker traditional academic background than may typically be expected of a college student. Consequently, an opportunity to use a familiar context such as Disney films offers a more level playing field where she is able to demonstrate strengths.

4. What have you learned about taking classes in college? Where are you most likely to be successful? To have difficulty? Will this affect your course selection and how you approach these courses?

At college, I have learned that managing time is extremely important. I regret not focusing enough on my studies in my first semester. Going forward, I will be more successful by starting to study and begin my assignments as early as possible. This way I have more time to understand the topic and not feel as anxious as I am doing it. If I start a paper too late, I am too nervous that I won't get it done on time, which makes it harder to focus.

One upside to my anxiety is that I would never be able to start a paper the day before it is due. I would be much too nervous! I will try to be more organized than I was my first semester. Because I know which subjects I enjoy, I will avoid taking anything math or science-related as best as I am able. If I do take math and science courses, I will need the input of academic advisors who may be more familiar with these classes and better able to recommend where I may be able to be more successful. At present, I have not become familiar enough with the professors or the departments to know which subjects and classes I should take in the future.

In this reflection, Michelle has begun formulating a plan of action. She is utilizing self-efficacy to move toward agency. She has identified a need to work on time management, one of the most important skills for all college students, particularly those with learning differences. Her comments about the upside of anxiety reframes an identified weakness as a perceived strength. In *My Age of Anxiety: Fear, Hope, Dread, and the Search for Peace of Mind* (2014), Scott Stossel notes that people with manageable anxiety often are high achievers who complete tasks conscientiously and carefully. Michelle recognized the utility of accessing support services in her selection of math and science classes with an awareness of the importance of finding a goodness of fit between how one learns and the approach of the instructor.

Project 3: This project may be developed jointly by the student and faculty member. Suggestions include an informal presentation/discussion with a graduate special education class, with an emphasis on suggesting effective teaching strategies; a future plan that incorporates the student's understanding of his or her learning disabilities with suggestions or strategies for further education and career planning; or a critical review of suggestions or recommendations in the student's evaluations. There are no specific guidelines for this part of the project, as it is based on a discussion of what would be best based on the student's knowledge of the self, the student's knowledge of his or her learning differences, and the student's self-awareness of the most effective way to represent and share this knowledge.

For this final project, Michelle agreed to be interviewed for a graduate class on lifespan issues of persons with disabilities. Her willingness to go public signifies an admirable level of self-acceptance and confidence. One purpose of the interview was the opportunity to inform the graduate candidates, who were primarily teachers, on her concepts of best practices. Her participation is a powerful form of self-advocacy with the intention of being a change agent.

❄ ❄ ❄

Teachers and parents should not rationalize that low self-concept, lack of confidence, defeatism, and so on are simply part of the territory of learning differences. Instead, we need to understand why these behaviors and feelings evolve. They are learned. We need to teach our students a different way of looking at themselves, the world around them, and their place in it. They can learn and inculcate attributes needed for transitioning to adulthood successfully, if we believe in our students and communicate it.

8 Breaking the Failure Cycle

Anyone who has never made a mistake has never tried anything new.

—Albert Einstein

The descent of many students into self-doubt and recrimination, frustration, despair, and learned helplessness are understandable reactions to repeated failure and criticism. Rather than reviewing common educational approaches used as interventions or remedies, this chapter presents a range of alternative therapeutic activities. Teachers and parents are encouraged to think outside the box and embrace nontraditional but empirically validated approaches, including guided positive imaging, game and skill activities, social skills training, meditation, stress and anxiety reduction, the arts, life skills, and new approaches to inclusion, all of which can be incorporated into the classroom and at home.

THE WINNING PICTURE

Talk to any good athlete. Before and during the game, they believe they can win. Some spend considerable amounts of money to work with sports psychologists who teach them to use positive visualizations. That is, they picture positive outcomes both at a micro and macro level. They expect success on the next muscle movement, the next inning or quarter, the whole game, the whole season, and even their whole careers.

Jamie Moyer, who at 49 became the oldest pitcher in major league history to win a game, turned his career around by controlling his thoughts on the mound (Moyer, 2014). He had bottomed out of baseball more than once not because his arm went bad but because he lost faith in himself.

Pitchers in a slump will admit that they become anxious before each pitch and start to worry that the next pitch will be a bad one. Self-doubt and negative thinking enter their outlook. They focus on what they do not want to happen rather than what they want to happen. They focus on the negative. If the pitcher says to himself, "I don't want to throw a ball," he more than likely will throw a ball. It gets even worse if the pitcher says, "I think I'm going to throw a ball." Successful athletes do not think they will fail. Unsuccessful ones think they will.

In school, kids who *think* they will fail, fail. Approaching a task with anxiety tends to create fear. Anxiety and fear are not necessarily counterproductive emotions. Walter Cannon (1932) coined the term for the choice that we usually make when we are afraid—*fight or flight*. Kids who have a history of failure may choose flight, which emerges as negative thinking or learned helplessness. On the other hand, a history of success encourages fight, in this case, a metaphor for rising to the challenge with a positive mindset.

The importance of positive visualization is clear in sports. A good pitcher not only thinks "I am going to throw a strike" but sees the trajectory and speed of the ball going over the plate before throwing it. Athletes also have a routine or ritual they go through just before a specific task. Watch a good foul shooter through the course of the game. The dribbles, the spinning, the set—they are all the same each time. Golfers perform what seems to be some kind of obsessive-compulsive disorder act before teeing off—taking a practice swing, waggling the club head by the ball, using the same sequence as they grip and rip.

These rituals are connected to picturing a positive outcome. They align the body movement, referred to as *muscle memory*, with the successful result. In a sense, the body and mind are rehearsing and remembering exactly what happens just before success is achieved. As the final motion begins, the mind lets go and the motion is automatic. Motorcyclist training courses teach riders to picture driving by a sudden obstacle rather than how to avoid it. It is a subtle difference, but it speaks volumes. We can train ourselves to anticipate creating positive results rather than worry about failing.

A tourist walking in midtown Manhattan asks a musician on the street, "How do I get to Carnegie Hall?" "Practice, man, practice." Virtually no success is achieved without practice. Visualization itself requires the hard work of rehearsing, incorporating new ideas, blocking old ones, and countless repetitions. A basketball player will not get better with free throws simply by picturing them. The player must be dedicated to a practice regimen, shooting hundreds of free throws every day. The player must have success based on hard work before the positive visualizations mean anything. And then, the player needs to practice visualizing the successful routine.

Nothing is easy about breaking the failure cycle. Parents and teachers wish that it were only a matter of telling kids with learning differences, "Think positively!" As with any teaching and learning experience, this transformation requires much more than lecturing or, worse, hectoring.

Most kids with learning differences have experienced failure cycles. They have little on which to build confidence. An intentional focus on what students are accomplishing rather than what they are not, what they are succeeding at rather than failing, slowly builds a degree of confidence. "Catch 'em being good" is especially important for students who are unsure of when they are good.

> ### Henry's Story
>
> The little things matter. Reinforcing positive social behavior is easy—as long as the parent or teacher is consciously tuned in. For example, our teenage daughter, who is a competitive runner, frequently butts into family conversations, simply interrupting a discussion with her own agenda. Last night at dinner, we tried to explain that interrupting was not a good way to enter a conversation. A few minutes later, when the rest of the family was discussing an obituary (long story) but focusing on all the wonderful things this individual had done, our daughter waited for a pause and said, "Speaking of life, running is very good for long-term health." Still her agenda but ingratiated in an appropriate (and clever) way. We immediately stopped to compliment her on her polite social manner. In the future, we hope she will visualize this moment when trying to enter the conversation and know her likelihood of positive acceptance is high.

We would do well to turn the world of school on its head. School is a place where failure is pointed out more often than it is in almost any other environment. *Failure* is a bad word. As we shall see, no one improves without failing. Nevertheless, no student wants to fail. As we pointed out in Chapter 5, instead of emphasizing mistakes on a paper or test, we have more opportunities to focus on what was successful. Further, we can help our students problem solve by tying in what they are doing right to figure out and correct what they are doing wrong. Students will not immediately or easily change their dispositions, but over time and with persistence, they may catch a foothold on believing they will be successful.

With a better degree of self-assurance (or even without) students with learning differences (especially adolescents) can practice positive visualizations on academic tasks. Testing is most amenable. When students know that a test is coming up, they can begin using class time to visualize what content is likely to be on the test. If they have notes, they should star or highlight these sections. Many students with learning differences have difficulty discerning the most relevant information. The teacher, parent, or other students may be able to help the student become more cognizant of what is expected.

For any sizeable test, the student should break down studying into three separate sessions. This approach is not only good time management but a good way to decrease fear, calm down, and build confidence. In the first session, the student primarily gets organized, making sure he or she is up-to-date on reading and related assignments, making a list of what to study, and looking over notes and chapter headings. The next session is devoted to review, not with an expectation of assimilating information but rather becoming familiar with it. This is also a good time to create flashcards with possible questions on one side and answers on the other—another type of visualization. The third session simulates the test through working with flashcards. Flashcards answered correctly go in one pile, and those answered incorrectly in another. After one round, the student repeats the process, drawing cards from the incorrect deck, until all the cards wind up in the correct pile. Working with peers is usually beneficial.

The visualization of the test becomes clearer if some of the sessions, particularly the last, take place in the classroom where the test will be administered. Aligning with the theory of state-dependent learning, this approach helps students build positive associations with the setting in which they will take the test. The classroom becomes much less intimidating when it is familiar.

On game day—a great metaphor to focus on winning, not losing—the student should arrive a few minutes before the test, if possible. Take a seat. Take deep breaths. Picture a positive outcome. You are in control. Positive results are not guaranteed, but the probability has increased.

SKILLS AND GAME SUCCESS

Before picturing positive results, we have to experience them. Effective visualizations are based in familiarity with winning. As we just mentioned, the greater challenge for students with learning differences is a lack of winning experiences. One of the overarching themes of this book is helping students understand and utilize their strengths as well as teaching them compensatory techniques. Clearly, organization, time management, planning, prioritizing, and so on form a foundation for improving academic outcomes. Strengthening interpersonal skills provides more satisfactory social interactions. Building relationships of trust and unconditional acceptance create a sense that one has a meaningful place and space in the world.

Let's go outside the traditional educational box and examine a few techniques that can pay off in ability to generate winning attitudes and expectations of success.

Do you think it is cool when someone can juggle? It is always impressive. It never gets a bad reaction. It is a difficult skill to learn, but most people can master it as long as they practice diligently. Students with learning differences who do not have significant fine or gross motor deficits can join this seemingly exclusive club. They need to learn to accept failure in the process, but for most, it is nothing like the failure of being humiliated and frustrated in a classroom setting. It's more a matter of dropping a ball, picking it up, and trying again. Each time they get a little closer, most kids are motivated to keep going, to persist. From the first time a child gets one rotation of three balls in the air, that child will be hooked. It is addicting. And what a great addiction—the desire to succeed!

Because it is an achievable skill, the student experiences a wonderful payoff. If you think it is cool to see someone juggle, imagine how cool it feels to be the juggler. The child has developed an area of strength. Equally important, the child can internalize what it took to get there—hard work. For some students, this is the beginning of reversing the perception that no matter how hard they work, they do not succeed. Internalizing that hard work leads to success is a critical life lesson. The quality of persistence grows from repeated experiences during which success may not come easily but it does come eventually. Persistence is one of the most commonly identified attributes of successful students and adults—with and without learning differences.

Another valuable life lesson emerges from continuing the process of discovering strengths, in this case, a strength that is immediately recognizable to the self and others. One does not have to become a consummate juggler to ascertain that it is a real ability. Instead, this strength adds to an overall repertoire, just one of the many strengths the individual possesses. This process incrementally boosts self-esteem, an attribute that is also essential for a healthy adulthood. Success in areas such as juggling may be the beginning of reframing.

Juggling is merely one example of breaking the failure cycle. Learning chess is another outlet where students who may have language difficulties find themselves in a nonverbal and highly conceptual environment. The game taps into the creative thinking and deep cognition that frequently go unrecognized in the typical classroom environment. It helps students to see a big picture when they must anticipate a series of steps to stay in the game.

Numerous articles ranging from scholarly research (e.g., Scholz et al., 2008) to a plethora of anecdotes extol the virtues of chess for students with learning differences. Rob Roy, a teacher of emotionally and educationally disadvantaged children, stated that he used chess as a way for them [the students] to learn and practice self-control. It was like turning on switches in their heads. You see the child looking at a problem, breaking it down, then putting the whole thing back together. The process involves recall, analysis, judgment, and abstract reasoning (Roy, 1989).

Chess may improve academic abilities not only in problem solving but in reading. As kids get more involved with chess, they gravitate toward reading about it. Reading in an area of high interest is practically guaranteed to improve reading skills. Interest is motivating, but it also builds a basic construct of reading: context. The more familiar we are with a particular subject, the better we will be able to pick up on the meaning of new words. We will be better at understanding the general idea of a passage. If we find ourselves agreeing or disagreeing with what we are reading, we are activating executive function.

As with juggling, chess teaches that persistence pays off. The majority of kids who learn chess do not internalize their losses as failures but rather as ways to figure out new strategies. They feel good about themselves and experience a tangible learning experience in which they can observe their cognitive skills expanding. They naturally engage in positive visualizations. They socialize—a not-inconsequential benefit derived from acquiring a recreational interest that lasts a lifetime.

Teachers and parents need to use common sense when encouraging students to tackle such pursuits. Although the positive value of juggling and chess is supported by research, not every student will find juggling or chess fulfilling. A child with learning differences who gets nothing but frustration and a sense of failure out of juggling or chess should not pursue it. But every individual has strengths. Every strength has a match with a fulfilling activity.

Discovering and engaging individual strengths should undergird teaching and parenting. It is infused throughout this book. Creating positive visualizations is another part of a success model. It is about having an optimistic and winning attitude and honing it into an intentional skill. The classroom experience of so many students with learning differences is not a fertile breeding ground for building the confidence that we all need to succeed throughout life. To build this attribute, students must be directed toward experiences that allow them to thrive. We need to put the brakes on the cycle of failure and spin it in the other direction. Success breeds success.

ACQUIRING SOCIAL SKILLS

Throughout the day, we are presented with opportunities for helping our students acquire valuable skills, especially social skills. Most kids pick up on social skills by seeing how others act. They adopt behaviors that are socially appropriate and get positive results. Students with learning differences often do not pick up social skills through observation. We have discussed social difficulties that result from deficits in nonverbal language processing. On top of that, students who have weaknesses with executive function do not process the relevant details and cause-and-effect phenomena around them. They do not integrate the many unwritten rules of efficacious social interaction.

Specific and direct instruction in social skills, which include nonverbal language communication, has a good track record in published research. That is, direct social skills instruction generally improves at least some characteristics of social behavior. Do the gains in social skills from direct instruction in school carry over to adulthood? We have much less information on the long-term effects of social skills training.

Social skills are important in childhood but critical in adulthood. Developing and using good social skills has a place in each theory of success discussed in Chapter 3.

Another way of gauging the impact of social skills in adulthood takes us back to Chapter 4 on outcomes. Studies from the 1980s on have consistently reported feelings of loneliness, less acceptance/more rejection, difficulties relating to others, and so on in adults with various learning differences such as attention deficit/hyperactivity disorder (ADHD) and autism spectrum. To make matters worse, these adults are largely unaware of what leads to such dissatisfaction. Researchers have surmised that social skills deficits are a root cause. Many adults with learning differences do not recognize their poor social skills and consequently do not associate them with social outcomes. It is especially hard to get out of this cycle.

Educators are seeing the value of including social skills instruction in the curriculum. Students with social skills issues deserve to learn teachable social skills. Individual Education Programs (IEPs) include room for social goals. Parents and teachers need to be mindful of their children's social/emotional states and seek ways to improve them when appropriate. Social skills can be taught and learned formally in class and informally outside of class. Learning about the importance of social skills and how to utilize them gives students tools for their adult survivor toolkit. None of us wants to see our children become lonely and sad adults with little hope on the horizon.

MEDITATION, NOT MEDICATION

The power of meditation has positive implications over the course of adulthood. Perhaps its most ubiquitous use is for dealing with stress and anxiety, which are endemic to living with learning differences. It literally changes body function; it allows the body to heal from being in the emergency mode caused by stress.

David Levy, a professor in the Information School at the University of Washington, begins his classes with a ten-minute meditation session. He helps train all his students to sit quietly and use meditation techniques before they begin the teaching and learning experience of the traditional college class. Dr. Levy has conducted experiments that show that meditation training helps individuals to be less fragmented in their work. They spend more time on discrete tasks and do not try to multitask. This not-so-startling finding has particular significance to many students with learning differences. The eminent Stanford psychologist Clifford Nass believes that individuals with attention deficits spread their attention over an inappropriately large span of stimuli. They are particularly susceptible to the ubiquitous environment of social media and multitasking.

Meditation takes many forms, from sitting silently in a calming environment to walking to mindful yoga movement techniques. The easiest form of meditation is to take a walk outside. Something as simple as taking a walk after 60 to 90 minutes of working, especially at the computer, relaxes the mind and helps the brain refresh itself at a neuropsychological level. It is important to go outside and take a stroll that connects as much as possible to the natural environment. Think how easy this would be to do during a school day.

Many teachers use short breaks, often as the need arises. Breaks are important. As we mentioned, a 10-minute break every 60 to 90 minutes, especially when people get outside, really helps the brain refresh itself. We used to call this *recess*. One teacher said to us,

> I am a HUGE fan of breaks! Not only for students with IEPs, but for any child who is getting frustrated and needs to take a breather! I can't tell you how many times I have had to walk away from a situation to gather my thoughts and take deep breaths—I feel this strategy can help anyone.

Teachers and parents who train themselves in simple meditation techniques will develop skills to serve students with learning differences who are transitioning to and making their way through adulthood. It is not difficult to incorporate Dr. Levy's approach in any classroom. It is useful for all students and does not single out those with learning differences.

Teachers and parents are often uncomfortable with the idea of using and teaching meditation techniques. Most of them are not complicated and require little more than asking students to close their eyes, stay silent, and breathe slowly and deeply. Encourage them to listen to silence.

The overwhelming amount of information that the digital age provides may be even more overwhelming to students with learning differences. They have everything in the world inundating them—sometimes self-imposed, sometimes intrusive. They do not have the psychological and emotional space to store it or process it. Their minds could become the next stars of the reality series, *Hoarders*. The remedy is obvious: Be silent. Disconnect.

Disconnect for at least a few hours a day from social media and digital communication. Social media can be addictive, distracting, and anxiety provoking. Multitasking (the phenomenon of doing a bunch of things poorly instead of one thing well) fragments centeredness. It generally makes us reactive rather than proactive.

Meditation holds an additional benefit for individuals with attention difficulties. For example, the teacher may ask students to close their eyes and picture a candle flame, serene brook, or other comforting image. Meditation requires intense concentration of attention that blocks out distracting thoughts while maintaining a singular focus. Neuropsychological research suggests that meditation reduces mental clutter and increases attention. Patterns in the brain change as an individual relaxes and enters a calm state. In this new state, the brain is better suited to function more efficiently.

> *Mindfulness* is a specific type of meditation. It activates executive functioning by paying attention to how we pay attention. Mindfulness training helps children to watch their minds working and to control their attention (British Psychological Society, 2013). Exercises are simple:
>
> - Becoming aware of the breath
> - Feeling the various physical sensations of an emotion
> - Noticing thoughts as they pass through the mind
> - Paying attention to all the sounds in the room
> - Noticing what happens in the body when there is stress
> - Watching the thoughts that arise when there is boredom
> - Feeling the stomach rise and fall with each breath
>
> (Association for Mindfulness in Education, 2013)

No one form of meditation is for everyone. Being aware of a variety of simple approaches will help teachers and parents suggest and participate in these ways to reduce stress and anxiety and increase attention and focus. Perhaps the most important caveat is that students enjoy meditation. It may take some work; one size may not fit all. But as research and experience make clear, all of us can take pleasure in and profit from some form of meditation.

STRESS, ANXIETY, AND OTHER REALITIES OF ADULTHOOD

Adulthood constantly requires multifaceted roles with a multitude of responsibilities. The impact of learning differences on the processes of adult development is unique to each individual. However, stress and anxiety are a pervasive part of adulthood for persons with learning differences (Morgan & Klein, 2000).

Blocking out extraneous or invasive thoughts is crucial for effective executive functioning. Individuals with learning differences often have trouble staying on both cognitive and physical tasks. They may feel besieged by stimuli, including their own thoughts. They cannot keep their mind on any one thing without dozens of other ideas bouncing around, each competing equally for attention. We usually think of this phenomenon as a characteristic of ADHD, but all of us are susceptible to thought distraction. We generally get a taste of this when we are worried, anxious, and stressed.

Students with learning differences have reasons to be anxious that do not necessarily disappear in adulthood. Poor adult readers may not be called upon to read out loud, but they may find themselves in a work or social situation that exposes their reading difficulties, such as being asked to read a menu or follow written directions. Finishing tasks on time, getting organized, going to new social events—adults with learning differences feel these anxiety-inducing events more acutely.

Being able to control or at least cope with invasive thoughts benefits students with learning differences in school and throughout life. A fine line distinguishes rumination from executive function. Students do need to be able to tap into the inner voice that allows thinking and behavior to be systematic and effective. Positive visualizations are also a type of executive function. As strict nonscientists, we will identify effective executive function as both proactive and focused. Reactive, negative, and worrisome thinking is unfocused and out-of-control. An example for most of us is racing thoughts as we try to get to sleep. We rehash anxieties from the day's events. Equally worrisome, these thoughts bounce around randomly. We do not feel in control.

Control separates effective executive functioning from wheel spinning. Consequently, students will find it beneficial to learn how to get in control of their own thoughts. Popular literature is replete with examples of how to slow down and control intrusive and unfocused thoughts. For example, deep and slow breathing, especially combined with a rehearsed metacognitive script of "focus," "clear mind," or "slow down," have a neuropsychological calming effect.

Such a technique is both meditative and metacognitive. The metacognitive aspect is to deploy a recognition that one's mind is off task and challenge one's own thinking. The paradox for many people with learning differences is that they may not be aware that they are unfocused and off task.

It is all too easy to miss or dismiss anxiety, worry, stress, and so on in children. We owe it to our children to listen to them and encourage them to talk honestly about their feelings. In addition to therapeutic value, talking about feelings during childhood raises awareness of a connection between their learning differences, their behaviors, and their emotional selves.

DON'T FORGET THE ARTS

How often do we find that we are unable to express our deepest emotions through the written or even spoken word? Being unable to communicate how we feel may lead to acting-out behaviors in both adults and children and contribute to anxiety, stress, and depression. The arts offer a way out. It is not uncommon to hear the phrase *healing through the arts*. Experiencing the arts soothes frayed ends and allows release. In an environment with a specially trained therapist, individuals learn to understand what their expressions mean. Art that reveals anger, frustration, or helplessness may be the first step in recognizing that those emotions exist.

The Individual Education Program (IEP) may include educational enrichment in music or art therapy. Staff or parents refer the student to a board-certified music therapist. The music therapist determines whether arts therapy is an appropriate service relevant to IEP objectives and goals. Arts therapy motivates some students to communicate better and acquire a more positive outlook. Academic benefits accrue from associating sounds or images with information and leads to increased retention and performance in the classroom. Arts therapy does not appear frequently on IEPs. There may be pushback. We advise parents and teachers to advocate forcefully and persistently for arts therapy when their students need to express and understand their emotions.

When a child gets applause from a group of adults (and peers), that child cannot feel bad about himself.

—Leo Eaton

Henry's Story

More than thirty years ago, I taught at a school created for students with learning differences. Our school was a truly special school. It was special because it offered about 50 six- to thirteen-year-old kids with learning differences an environment that recognized strengths, taught compensatory strategies, and, most importantly, sent those children a message that they were whole and good—not the bruised, self-conscious, and marginalized kids some of them had already become.

Even though our school was small and extracurricular opportunities were limited, it was important for our students to have the same out-of-class experiences as any other students. We started a school newspaper—literally cut and pasted together with photos and stenciled graphics, run off at Kinkos (seems like ancient history). I began a glee club, with a focus on *glee*. Ten to twenty students would sing whatever they wanted to sing, the favorite being the chorus to a popular Billy Joel song: "You may be right. I may be crazy!" They sang—and laughed and shouted and stomped. They were celebrating all the parts of themselves that had nothing to do with their learning differences.

I started a boys' break dance club. Remember break dancing? To see a bunch of often-insecure and bickering boys standing in a circle, cheering and clapping for whoever danced in the middle was a powerful moment. Some of these boys did not exactly move like Mick Jagger. It didn't matter. The other boys still clapped and cheered. For the boy who dared to go to the center of the circle and put it on the line, he had freed himself from all the weight that normally filled his life. Now he soared on affirmation and the sheer pleasure of physical self-expression.

At a screening of *Arts and the Mind* (a PBS documentary), Leo Eaton, the Emmy award-winning filmmaker, concluded the presentation with this observation—the arts are vital for children both in neuropsychological development (how all the circuits in the brain process and respond) and in basic self-concept and a sense of well-being. The arts are critical to cognitive development, a sense of autonomy, and risk-taking. Exposing children and adults to participation in the arts does not have to be intentionally therapeutic. Good things almost always happen.

Filmmaking is another means of expression. Many high schools offer film and video production. Students with learning differences often fit well in this milieu, where skills other than reading, writing, or math become essential. Media production is an ever-expanding market. Familiarity with this area provides practical training as well as psychological and social benefits.

Art forms can be combined with academics. For many students with learning differences, they connect to different subject areas in new and helpful ways. Kelly is an eighth-grade teenager with dyslexia and a talented singer. She reads at approximately a fourth-grade level despite an oral vocabulary level at the tenth-grade level. She has had years of systematic reading instruction but has yet to apply it to her learning.

When Kelly entered educational therapy, she continued her systematic reading program. In order to make the learning more engaging, her therapist bridged the lessons to music lyrics. Each week, Kelly would share what songs she was listening to on iTunes and print out the lyrics. Using the lyrics, Kelly would first highlight every place she noted words with the grapheme/phoneme connections she had previously learned. She would also note words that she would not have known how to read had she not known the words to the song already. From there, she would sing the song while reading the lyrics. Because she knew the words, she would read fluently, similar to the approach used in a repeated reading method, a well-researched fluency technique.

By incorporating word walls and applying her learning to her assigned school texts, Kelly eventually began to recognize more grapheme/phoneme patterns and her reading ability gradually increased. Moreover, her fluency increased. She still uses audio-based textbooks and extended time and is now rapidly improving her reading in a software-based reading program, Virtual Reading Coach. Music, however, continues to play a critical role in her reading intervention program.

Arts and the Mind speaks powerfully to the importance of exposure to and participation in the arts for students and how this cannot be separated from any area of the curriculum. Many administrators (and, consequently, teachers) in this era of standardized tests and measuring student achievement feel compelled to stay within the box and look at art as superfluous and distracting from their mission. They could not be more wrong. Are the arts important for persons with learning differences? No—they are essential.

LIFE SKILLS

What images does a life skills class call to mind? The vast majority of these classes are part of the special education program, usually in high school. They typically support students with moderate to profound intellectual disabilities, autism, and other developmental disabilities. It is not the type of class a student on a general academic curriculum would expect to attend.

A degree of life skills instruction is equally important for virtually all students. Home economics, fundamentals of technology, financial management, and other skills courses are part of most high school curricula. Students with learning differences profit from these classes. However, many students, with and without learning differences, need more preparation in basic life skills. These skills include

- cooking,
- nutrition,
- exercise,

- cleaning,
- laundry,
- storing and organizing,
- hygiene,
- self-care,
- personal safety,
- making a bed (and washing linens),
- using transportation,
- ordering in a restaurant,
- basic social skills,
- basic mechanics,
- and on and on and on.

These skills are typically taught in special education pull-out classes, although some of these tasks are relevant for any student. Rather than sending students with diagnosed disabilities to special education pull-out programs, teachers and parents need to find ways to integrate these skills into the curriculum as well as daily life. Most of these skills are related to functional home skills, giving parents plenty of opportunities to address them. Children with learning differences may not learn simply by observing. They need specific guidance. The effort must be intentional. It is not easy. As parents ourselves, we do not teach all the tasks necessary for independent living, even though we know better. We plead guilty to enabling rather than instructing, because it's easier! Take stock of the basic living skills needed for a successful transition to adulthood.

At the other end of the curriculum, instruction in some life skills may be too cursory to stick for students with learning differences. For example, finance management in a high school class typically addresses balancing a checkbook. Most students can handle this task in the classroom. Not all are able to generalize it to their personal lives. In addition, balancing a checkbook is only one of the many tasks needed to control personal finances. Managing finances is a high-level skill and eludes many people without disabilities. The percentage of Americans who are in debt because they do not manage their finances well is very high, and impulsive behavior is a factor. Budgeting also is a very conceptual process that involves making predictions based on analysis.

Sarfraj Rathod, a writer for the education and business website *Voniz*, advocates adding higher-level life skills for all high school students (2014). Not surprisingly, we agree with him, starting with his recommendation for managing finances. Most high schools do not explore how to save, spend, and effectively manage the home/business startup. They do not prepare students to manage long-term finances, from building equity to preparing for retirement. It is not realistic to expect high schools to include this level of detail for all students; parents must take the initiative to discuss and prepare for these high-level life demands.

In Chapter 4, we met Ray Peterson, a young adult with learning differences who struggled to find a good job. His poor interviewing skills left him stranded. Although high schools give a number of students resume-building and interview experiences, the process for students with learning differences may require more analytical breakdown, more feedback, and more instruction.

OUTSIDE-THE-BOX INCLUSION

In an era of inclusion, students with learning differences spend most if not all of their time in general education classes. Providing extra time in class is a reasonable and logical accommodation for students who process information at a slower rate. But it presents a dilemma to teachers. Most students do not move at this pace and may become bored and disengaged. It does not make sense to adopt a singular model of instruction when classes have such diversity of learning styles and needs.

Using a mix of online technology, small group instruction, independent learning, and interactive hands-on experiences can free teachers to be more responsive to individual needs. Schools increasingly provide online tools. Teachers can augment these programs with free online software. In a flash, teachers can implement personalized lessons and easily monitor progress, which is automatically processed through the software. Frequent checks of how students are doing (or formative assessment) allow teachers to adjust instructional approaches and materials. Some programs spell out the types of changes that are most sensible.

Combining online teaching tools with traditional face-to-face instruction is referred to as a *blended class*. Some students may work in small groups following an online lesson. Some work independently. Some need a lot of personal assistance. It takes effort and energy. We leave it to experts to write in depth about blended instruction and the use of online resources. Websites abound with a dizzying array of tips, guidelines, lesson plans, assessments, and interactive software.

Technology does not replace good teaching. Overreliance on technology disengages teachers from their most important roles. Effective blended instruction requires a willingness to evaluate the extent to which methods are meeting goals and to let go and move on when online tools are not doing the job.

When done right, blended instruction is a true Universal Design for Learning. It offers teachers a much more efficient way to work with their diverse students. Instead of leveling the playing field, it creates multiple fields and multiple games. Students with learning differences get greater and better opportunities to learn in ways that are more natural and native for them. They express their acquisition and use of new information and skills through more authentic assessment.

IT'S NOT THE PROGRAM—IT'S YOU

The tips included in this chapter represent merely a few of the concepts about creative ways to break the failure cycle. The key word is *creative*. Arbitrarily pulling some of these approaches out of a hat will produce mixed results at best. Close attention to the types of difficulties students with learning differences face should guide the direction of the intervention. We hope we have provided useful ways to work with students, but we do not see this chapter as simply adding tools to the proverbial "teacher's toolbox." Rather, we encourage teachers and parents to use initiative and creativity to help students. Visualization, meditation, arts, life skills— these are not typically programmatic. They depend more on teachers and parents finding opportunities to integrate them inside and outside the classroom. If you want your children and students with learning differences to find novel ways to steer themselves to and through adulthood, get outside your comfort zone. Think outside the box.

9 Teaching the Attributes of Successful Adults With Learning Differences

Resilience is all about being able to overcome the unexpected. Sustainability is about survival. The goal of resilience is to thrive.

—Jamais Cascio

The authors have worked with hundreds of college students with and without learning differences and utilized research and best practices to help them take control of their academics and successfully manage the demands of college life and beyond. We present these recommendations to help teachers, parents, and students with learning differences find the path to adult success. We conclude with some thoughts on self-advocacy, the characteristic underlying autonomy, control, and success of children and adults with learning differences.

SEVEN ATTRIBUTES OF SUCCESSFUL ADULTS WITH LEARNING DIFFERENCES

Young adults with learning differences can achieve career success and personal satisfaction. A combination of effective self-advocacy and specific life skills can make significant differences in adult outcomes. *Exceeding Expectations: Successful Adults with Learning Disabilities* (Reiff, Gerber, & Ginsberg, 1997) provided a focus on what adults with learning differences can do rather than what they cannot do. These characteristics do not differ wildly from those found in the models of success previously described in Chapter 4, but they do draw out specifics relevant to individuals with learning differences. By informing our teaching with the predictable processes that lead to success, we will be teaching for the lifespan. This chapter presents recommendations and examples of the seven attributes in *Exceeding Expectations* and approaches culled from the authors' research on successful adults with learning differences.

Successful adults with learning differences take control of their lives, a process that begins in adolescence and continues in adulthood. The experience of growing up with learning differences often leads to a loss of psychological control. From the interviews of a relatively large group of high-achieving adults in *Exceeding Expectations*, seven attributes led them to gain control of their lives and career success.

1. Desire

Successful adults with learning differences have the drive and desire to achieve. In many cases, they want to show the world that they can do it, whatever *it* is. They may still have some anger toward all the people who told them they were not going to make it, but they channel their anger into a force of will. How do we find positive ways to build and foster a desire to succeed in our student?

Parents and teachers know students must be motivated to succeed but are unsure of specific motivational methods. One group of educators, however, is all about motivation—coaches. Perhaps we should take something from their playbook. A good coach looks for skills in players and reinforces them. Effective coaches challenge players and even make them angry. However, they make sure to build up their players' self-confidence so that each player has the emotional resources to respond to sometimes-fiery criticism.

Role models of successful adults with learning differences inspire students. We do not have to rely on celebrities. Every community has professionals of various stripes who learn differently. Many are public about their learning differences and interested in advocacy. Invite these adults to your school or classroom. Knowing that success comes in areas other than sports and entertainment opens up new avenues of aspirations and goals for many students.

Nothing succeeds like success. Success in an activity can act as a foundation for building the desire to succeed. As we have discussed, opportunities for success abound inside and outside the classroom. And remember to give plenty of praise!

2. Goal Orientation

The adults in this study didn't just have goals; they had goal plans. They broke the big picture into little ones and learned how to do each step at a time, each step coming closer to achieving the goal. Students who are organized and use time management and study routines are practicing goal orientation. Because being organized is often more difficult for people with learning differences, making use of organization and time management approaches can be the difference between success and failure. Get organized. Manage your time. Don't let time manage you.

Difficulties with planning and organizing can undermine meeting objectives and goals. Task analysis helps students to break down goals to a series of steps, each of which is attainable. A key element in goal orientation lies in the ability to make reasonable and logical predictions. Students with learning differences can increase the accuracy of predicting through systematic instruction, especially in areas of reading comprehension (Palincsar & Brown, 1984). Opportunities undoubtedly exist for applying such systematic instruction to predicting possible career paths.

High school students need to begin planning for the post-school world. They cannot make reasonable and attainable choices if they are unaware of opportunities that exist. Use of instruments such as *The Self-Directed Search* (Holland, 1994) encourage students to plan vocational goals. They compare "Occupational Daydreams" with the results of the inventory, analyze the variables used in determining the results, and reflect on the relation of their "daydreams" to those variables.

3. Reframing

Reframing is a psychological process whereby we are able to change our perception about ourselves—in this case, meaning that our children and students see their learning differences as something positive rather than negative. They can jump-start this process by focusing on their strengths. Tell them, "You have plenty of strengths, even if you haven't given them much thought. Write them down. Think about your weaknesses, too. But consider how you use your strengths to compensate for your weaknesses. Have you become a more empathetic person because of the difficulties you've endured? There you go. Turn the lemon into lemonade. Own your learning differences, and you control the route to your success."

Owning learning differences involves recognizing, accepting, and understanding one's learning style. The individual begins to think about how to plan and act based on these steps to self-actualization. We have consistently emphasized the importance of helping students learn about their strengths and weaknesses, what works best and what does not work, where they are uncomfortable and where they are not, and when to ask for help and when not to. Reframing develops an internal locus of control, an antidote to learned helplessness. Reframing makes goals clearer and failure more realistic and less threatening. No one is perfect. No one is hopeless. If we look at ourselves honestly, we can avoid pitfalls of blame, excuses, and lack of accountability. Equally important, we develop strategies to achieve desirable outcomes. More than most of us, people with learning differences need to evaluate the intersection of their learning styles and their goals to be prepared for navigating a world that is not always fitted for them.

Reframing takes many shapes and forms. When one adult's fiancée read him the riot act about his inappropriate social behaviors, that experience shook him out of his social obliviousness and motivated him to take greater responsibility for his social actions. Sometimes we may need to read the riot act to our students and children as a reality check. Confrontation need not be adversarial but can instead be a systematic effort to develop recognition, understanding, and acceptance of learning differences without buying into pity or commiseration. Challenging confidence-building experiences can be used to facilitate the reframing process. For example, programs such as Outward Bound challenge the individual to go beyond previously held expectations with the intention that the individual will confront and overcome personal weaknesses. Peer support groups also facilitate reframing. Sharing issues makes it easier for many students to deal with their own concerns and discover that they are not alone with their problems and struggles. They may learn new methods for coping with specific academic demands, thereby broadening their understanding and plan of action. Finally, counseling is an excellent vehicle to help some students reframe their learning differences. The one-to-one interaction provides a safe harbor for exploring personal issues.

4. Persistence

Successful people with learning differences work hard, very hard. We call this trait *persistence*. At work, these are the people who are first in and last out. They never give up. Failure is not a stopping point; it simply means looking for a new way to solve a problem.

Thomas Edison may have been the biggest failure of all time. Do you know how many failures it took to invent the lightbulb—or any of his inventions? Thousands, literally. He said that getting it wrong was not a failure; it simply helped him eliminate something that did not work. But here is something special about people with learning differences: Successful adults told us that they learned to work hard when they were young. Why? They did not have a choice. They had to work harder to earn Cs than their smart friends did to earn As. It was frustrating and, at times, painful. However, as adults, they found they were ready to outwork anyone. They knew how to walk that walk. And their smart friends who never had to crack a book in high school? Not so much.

Students with learning differences must acquire the ability to cope with failure. Special education has often focused solely on success-assured activities. We must be careful not to shortchange students by shielding them. Supporting them but allowing them to struggle builds a heightened sense of resilience, determination, and persistence. Failure is a natural part of growing, learning, and achieving. Perhaps the problem lies in an institutionalized attitude that failure is bad, a sign of weakness and incompetence. We need constantly to remind our students that nothing is wrong with failing as long as they keep trying. As we will see, self-advocacy opens the door to showing that persistence pays off.

5. Goodness of Fit

Persons who are successful find jobs and careers that maximize their strengths and minimize their weaknesses. They also like—no, love—what they do. This alignment is called *goodness of fit*. Anyone will do better in a situation that capitalizes on personal strengths, but this is even more important to persons with learning differences. Our advice: Let's face it; there are things that simply are really difficult for you. Don't worry about it. Instead, discover your strengths and learn how and where you can apply them. Find out what you love to do. Talk to a career counselor who can assess your strengths, weaknesses, and interests and suggest jobs that fit.

Adults with learning differences find goodness of fit in some surprising ways. A dyslexic dentist told us that after years of seeing letters and words backwards, working through a dental mirror came naturally and easily. A writer who publishes in *Reader's Digest* shared that he writes at about a fourth-grade reading level—which is exactly what the magazine looks for. As we saw with Coller in Chapter 4, she chose her specialization because the medical textbooks in her field had the most pictures, which were critical to her learning and understanding.

The concept of *goodness of fit* has immediate relevance to students with learning differences. Goodness of fit ranges from selection of courses in high school to choosing a major in college to finding employment. It is an outcome of reframing. Understanding and planning for strengths and weaknesses facilitates making good decisions about finding environments where their strengths are maximized, weaknesses are minimized, and interest is heightened.

We should also consider using simulation activities to help students increase their sense of fit. We need to involve students in developing checklists or inventories detailing positives and negatives for a given choice. Role playing is also effective. Acting out a scenario where a person with significant spelling problem gets a job waiting on tables facilitates reflection on what type of jobs will be comfortable or uncomfortable.

6. Learned Creativity

Successful adults with learning differences have developed a repertoire of tricks and strategies that compensate for their weaknesses, a phenomenon we call *learned creativity*. Successful students figure out special approaches that help with demands at school. Perhaps they've learned how to get what they need from a chapter or book without reading the whole thing. Maybe they have learned a unique way of doing math problems—not the teacher's way, but *their way*—and it works. These skills play into other areas of life.

A lawyer with learning differences had a great memory for faces but had trouble remembering names. He kept folders of clients with the pictures and names of each one as the primary identification. A federal police officer who had trouble spelling back in the days before computer self-correction would call the operator and ask how to spell a word. It always worked. We highly recommend keeping a basic to-do list, maybe of things that other people can keep in their heads but might pop out of yours. Know yourself, think about how to be your best, and be creative. Talk to your friends with learning differences and share your stories. You'll be amazed at what you learn—and what you teach your friends.

Success for individuals with learning differences requires creative and innovative ways of accomplishing tasks. Activities in school with numerous options for completion stimulate divergent thinking. Allowing students to choose their own mode of presentation represents a best practice of Universal Design for Learning.

Guidance from teachers and parents and interaction with peers provide excellent opportunities for students to discuss how they cope with academic and other demands. Students may be able to utilize strategies that others employ or become inspired to devise their own unique approaches. They can brainstorm ways to problem solve. Students may discuss how different methods can still generate the same solution and create the approach that works best for them.

7. Positive Social Network

Hillary Rodham Clinton said, "It takes a village," and she could not have been more right when it comes to being a successful adult with learning differences. Everyone needs a support system or a *positive social network*. The people we interviewed had family, friends, and coworkers who understood their issues and helped them make their way through the world. Spouses wrote thank-you notes and holiday cards for their dyslexic partners. Employees with learning differences worked with their colleagues to divvy up tasks; they did not dump stuff they could not do on others (not a smart approach) but rather worked interdependently and collaboratively to best make use of their strengths and abilities. We also noticed that so many successful adults had mentors, guiding forces who modeled positive behaviors and pushed and supported their protégées to be successful.

Who is part of your student's social network? Probably parents. For someone who is in a committed relationship, the spouse or significant other may be the go-to person. Does the individual have a mentor? It is essential to make use of these relationships, to be assertive and take action, and to find people who can help. Individuals with learning differences cannot be victims or only takers. They need to offer something in return. This is where the rubber meets the road in owning one's learning differences.

Parents and teachers should act as the center of a support system. Not every teacher is likely to be helpful, but most of us have had one or two teachers who offered tremendous support and understanding. They made all the difference. As much as parents are often the bedrock of security for their children, many inadvertently communicate expectations that create stress and pressure on their child with learning differences. As we have said, support your children in pursuing *their* direction in life, which is not necessarily yours. As with building the preceding attributes, peer support groups are part of a positive social network. Students will be able to support each other under the proactive guidance of teachers or counselors. Students may be able to profit from support group activities where the development of mutual empathy and concern serves to provide a safe harbor and forum for dealing with difficult issues. In this environment, students can learn that asking for help and support is acceptable; conversely, they will receive feedback if their needs become overly dependent.

We have identified these seven attributes as individual processes. In practice, they do not operate individually but interactively. For example, having particular goals combined with a positive sense of how to use one's abilities tends to increase desire to achieve, persistence, learned creativity, and positive social networks that contribute to goodness of fit. In fact, the effectiveness of any one attribute may depend on the effectiveness of another. Hard work and persistence are traits found in all models of success. However, persistence results in frustration if the person with learning differences does not have a good sense of his or her strengths and weaknesses, of how to set reasonable goals and break down the tasks, of goodness of fit, of creative compensations, and of a good support network. Countless other permutations of such interactions exist; interaction is crucial to the successful adaptability for persons with learning differences. Integrated approaches will result in learning experiences that more accurately reflect the processes used in attaining success.

IT COMES DOWN TO THIS

In the course of this book, we have discussed a number of theories on how people become successful adults. We have applied such models to children and adults with learning differences, particularly in this chapter. Children, adolescents, and young adults can learn these types of skills. As we have seen, there are countless ways to improve the likelihood of success in adulthood for students with learning disabilities.

To make a successful transition, one skill—self-advocacy—is the first among equals. Self-advocacy is critical for negotiating the transitions from adolescence to adulthood. The support systems of childhood begin to drop away. Parents and teachers stress accountability and personal responsibility. By adulthood, there are no more excuses, no more fallbacks. Adults are expected to be responsible for taking charge of their lives. Self-advocacy is inherently linked to successful transition.

Effective self-advocacy for persons with learning differences must be tied to other traits of success. It begins with a recognition of being different. From that recognition comes self-acceptance, understanding, and, eventually, a sense of how to work with one's unique strengths and weaknesses. Self-advocacy means knowing how to work with the system, how to challenge it when necessary, and how to ask for and get help while being as independent, autonomous, and individual as possible.

In this last section, we present a guide for building self-advocacy skills in children and adolescents with learning differences. We end with a personal narrative of self-advocacy in action.

SELF-ADVOCACY

Chambers and Ofiesh (2015) describe the importance of teaching students how to request accommodations and explicitly instruct students in the areas of self-awareness, self-understanding of learning differences, setting goals, self-advocacy at Individual Education Programs (IEPs) and/or transition meetings, engaging supportive adults, and accessing community resources. For further information and tips on increasing self-advocacy, please consult the websites for Advocating Change Together (http://www.selfadvocacy.org) and Self Advocates Becoming Empowered (http://www.sabeusa.org). Chambers and Ofiesh (2015) offer some general tips for cultivating self-advocacy and self-awareness. These recommendations, listed in the box below, were originally designed for individuals in special education. With the exception of requesting accommodations (which are by law provided only to those with IEPs or 504 plans), the tips can easily be applied to individuals with learning differences across all settings.

Self-Advocacy Instruction

Requesting Accommodations

Students should be assigned an advisor or case manager who can help coordinate the accommodations and recommendations into the academic program as well as help the student know how to locate the necessary people on campus who will provide and implement the services. In keeping with the literature on teaching independence, the advocate should help the student assume increased responsibility for expressing and securing his educational needs.

As a student transitions from middle school to high school, he or she should have practice identifying accommodations and practicing how he or she would explain them to his or her teachers. Include role playing in the student's practice until he or she feels comfortable doing this with no prompts and/or supports. Prior to having the student request accommodations from a teacher, model and practice helpful techniques to address the teacher, such as

- describing the student's learning difference and how it relates to each accommodation,
- maintaining eye contact with the teacher, and
- having a friendly tone of voice.

The student should ask the teacher for an appointment to discuss accommodations. Work with the student to identify optimal versus inopportune times to request

(Continued)

(Continued)

an appointment and to practice asking for an appointment and briefly explaining the reason for the appointment. For example, "I'd like to make an appointment with you to discuss my learning differences and some accommodations that would help me be successful in your class. I'd feel more comfortable if we could talk about it when other students aren't around. When would be a good time for you to meet?"

Explain the purpose of accommodations to the student. Avoid using educational jargon and make sure to use language that the student can understand. Make sure the student's general education teachers are aware of his or her learning difference and accommodations so that they are prepared to implement them.

Schedule periodic meetings with the student and his or her teachers to review the effectiveness of accommodations.

Instruction

Self-Awareness

Students should understand that people are not born with innate learning styles but that different people often find that they learn more efficiently through different methods and that these methods change according to the person's level of schooling, learning situation, and the tasks he or she is expected to accomplish. For example, some people find that taking notes during a lecture helps them to monitor their understanding; others find it difficult to take notes and focus on the lecture simultaneously, so they benefit from having a copy of someone else's notes. Ensure that the student understands clearly the nature of his or her difficulties. Teach the student ways in which he or she may use his or her strengths to compensate for weaknesses.

Use pictures to show how the brain processes information. For example, when explaining how working memory can impact a person's ability to follow oral directions, a teacher can use a picture or model of the brain, multiple strips of paper with individual words and sentences on them, and paper arrows pointed toward the brain to show how the brain can become overwhelmed with too much new information coming in at once. For some individuals, pictures can help communicate learning processes much more effectively than words.

Talk to the student about his or her IEP, 504 Plan, or school/independent evaluation and ensure that he or she knows how the recommendations relate to the specific learning difference (or differences) and foster strengths. For example, explain to the student that he or she receives extended time on tests because, although the student knows the test content, he or she reads slowly and/or needs more time to process information.

Help the student develop a clear understanding of the types of tasks that are easy for him or her versus those that are difficult. Help the student explore the types of courses and career options that are most in line with his or her unique talents. Have the student take an aptitude and interest inventory to identify some of the careers that might suit him or her best.

Give the student specific praise about strategies he or she has used successfully. Students need to understand what behaviors make them successful learners.

Understanding Learning Differences

Teach the student about learning differences in general. Explain the student's specific learning differences, discuss the fact that other people have similar differences, and explain how the techniques and interventions that have been selected will address his or her present needs. Also be sure to discuss the student's areas of cognitive, academic, and social strengths.

Discuss with the student how all people are unique and have areas in which they excel and areas in which they struggle. Help the student understand his or her own individuality so that the student is able to make an accurate, noncritical, and honest self-appraisal.

Self-Advocacy at IEP and/or Transition Meetings

Help the student develop a self-advocacy plan for either work or school, including a list of accommodations and/or modifications he or she will need. In preparation for this, help the student prepare to run his or her own IEP meetings. Part of the preparation should include a self-evaluation of academic and personal strengths, areas to improve, and vocational or educational goals. If allowable, the student should also set the date for his or her IEP meeting and send out notices. Subsequent to the IEP meeting, help the student monitor his or her progress toward the goals and objectives.

Prior to the student's IEP (or transition) meeting, meet with the student to discuss his or her learning differences and increase the student's awareness of his or her own challenges. Also discuss what helps the student cope with his or her challenges (e.g., accommodations). For example, the student may say, "It's hard for me to read and I read slowly, so it helps me when the teacher lets me read the sentence to myself first before she calls on me to read it out loud." Coach the student through a mock IEP meeting to help him or her prepare.

Have the student actively participate in his or her annual IEP meeting by following the Self-Advocacy Strategy (Van Reusen, Bos, Schumaker, & Deshler, 2007). This includes providing an inventory of skills and challenges during the IEP meeting, actively asking questions, actively responding to questions, and summarizing his or her IEP goals. More information about the Self Advocacy Strategy can be found at http://sim.kucrl.org/products/details/self-advocacy-strategy.

Prior to the student's IEP meeting, have the student create his or her inventory, including his or her learning strengths, needed areas of improvement, academic and career goals (if applicable), and classroom accommodations and/or modifications.

Review with the student productive techniques of asking and responding to questions, such as having a pleasant tone of voice, having an open body posture, and asking questions to clarify anything he or she may not understand.

(Continued)

(Continued)

Finally, have the student create a summary of the academic goals listed on his or her IEP.

Encourage the student to use self-advocacy skills to prepare for transition out of high school. Have the student identify career goals and what he or she would need to do to achieve those goals. Some topics to consider would be postsecondary education versus vocational training and the process of pursuing employment (e.g., filling out a job application or attending an interview).

Encourage the student to identify social skills that would be beneficial in and out of school. These skills could include introducing oneself, accepting and giving compliments and criticism, asking for help, working well with others, and making plans and following through.

As part of the transition meeting, help the student and his or her parents understand that colleges and universities will ask the student to indicate whether he or she has a disability and, if so, they should provide documentation that supports the student's requests for accommodation. The college disabilities support provider will interact directly with the student, not with the parents, so that student will be responsible for obtaining services and legal protections. Discuss with the student how this process will work and the role that he or she will play in securing the needed accommodations.

Engage Supportive Adults

In order to become a self-advocate, the student will need continuous support and encouragement from knowledgeable adults, parents, and teachers who will support him or her in developing both academic and vocational goals. It is important to communicate to key adults in the student's life the need to encourage the student to be active in his or her own self-advocacy.

Encourage parents, teachers, and mentors to support both academic and nonacademic areas so that the individual has many opportunities to be successful. Do not remove involvement in successful nonacademic areas (e.g., sports) as a way to improve academics. Provide opportunities for individuals to access mentors in areas of interest in order to maintain a love of learning and have role models for success.

Foster collaboration between general and special education teachers. General education teachers should receive a written snapshot of a student that includes the nature of the student's disability, how it impacts learning, and what the key interventions are that the teacher can implement in class.

Often, parents and students with learning differences become accustomed to school-based support and are unaware of services in the community that an individual would benefit from during and after high school. Teachers can provide the student and his or her parents with a wealth of information regarding community services available to adults with learning differences (e.g., attention deficit/hyperactivity disorder [ADHD] coaching, study skills, reading remediation). In fact, it is recommended that preservice teachers identify and begin to collect this information during their teacher preparation. This activity is useful for many teachers who themselves are not aware of how many community resources are available. Information should include agencies and services for adults with learning differences regarding eligibility requirements and available services.

As we foster resilience and self-efficacy, teachers must be mindful to include pathways to further education, participation in recreation/leisure activities, and volunteer and work opportunities. Only with this whole-person approach can teachers truly prepare individuals for adulthood. Some individuals with learning differences may benefit from consultation with a vocational transition specialist to coordinate school services, related services, and adult services in the community.

Source: Adapted from Chambers, A., & Ofiesh, N. (2015). Self-Advocacy. In N. Mather & L. E. Jaffe (Eds.), *Reports and recommendations for the Woodcock-Johnson IV*. Hoboken, NJ: Wiley.

Henry's Story

Not every student with learning differences will achieve this degree of self-advocacy. On the other hand, attending parent-teacher conferences for our daughter, C, who is currently a sophomore in a relatively large public school, provided an affirmation of what some basic forms of self-advocacy can accomplish. In a couple of conferences, the first thing her teachers discussed was her visible self-advocacy. C had been taking the initiative to ask questions if she did not understand something. She did not stop there. If the teacher did not give her a response that worked for her, she pointed that out and asked again. Her teachers were not put off by her persistence. Her extra effort to get on top of the material impressed her teachers. She started to be aware that she was creating a positive cycle. The positive reaction from her teachers gave her the confidence not only to ask questions but to participate in class discussions.

Over the years, we worked with C to build advocacy skills, which required building self-esteem and confidence. Beginning in fourth grade, we began discussing attention deficit/hyperactivity disorder (ADHD) and language-learning difficulties with her. She initially pushed back. She did not want to be identified as a kid with ADHD. She recognized that other kids with ADHD struggled in school and were frequently looked down upon. We explained to her that nothing was wrong with her, but she would have to focus on using her strengths and compensating in the areas that were difficult.

We began by working with her to build a strong work ethic. We asked her to face a reality of needing to work harder than many other students to achieve the level of success she wanted. Homework that took 30 minutes for her classmates often took 90 minutes for her. We all agreed that it wasn't fair, but it was necessary. To reinforce and support

(Continued)

(Continued)

her, her mother monitored and helped with her homework every day. If mom was willing to put in the effort, C began to be willing as well. Through sixth and seventh grade, they built a routine: Take a break and chill after school until 4:00. Homework together for the next 90 minutes. Chill and have dinner. She usually completed her homework in this time, but occasionally, she needed to put in a little time after dinner.

She was succeeding in school. She did not have the best grades in class, but she felt the equal of her classmates. We also began to talk about how the ability to work hard would give her an edge as she grew older. We shared research—in a developmentally appropriate way—that showed that adults with learning differences who were successful credited their work ethic as a major factor of success. They also related that they felt better prepared for adult life than many of their peers who had not been accustomed to working hard nor working through failure.

Through eighth grade, C had been enrolled in an extremely small parochial school, with only six students in her graduating class. The next step was to enter ninth grade at the local public high school, where the freshman class alone numbered more than 400. The thought of such a transition was somewhat unnerving to us, but C was confident that she would be able to handle her new environment and focused on the positives of playing sports, being able to create a wider social circle, and jumping in to a greater range of educational opportunities.

During C's eighth grade year, we began a transition process. Much of it involved screening, testing, identification, and recommendation process as outlined through the Individuals with Disabilities Education Act (IDEA 2004) and the local school system. In order to receive services through the IDEA, labels are a big deal; (specific) learning disabilities are one of them. Criteria for the classification of learning disabilities remain locked into discrepancy formulas (see discussion in Chapter 1). She did not meet the identification for a specific learning disability and consequently would not be entitled to an IEP. We were apprehensive. Having observed her from an early age and all through her schooling, we knew that she displayed characteristics of language learning differences. Reading, writing, and particularly spelling have been and continue to be difficult.

The evaluation team concluded that she has ADHD, which was not recognized under IDEA. Instead, she qualified for a 504 plan, essentially an "IEP lite." She would be able to use extended time for tests and papers. Equally important, the plan included useful and relevant instructional recommendations for her teachers.

After we received the 504 plan, we reviewed it with C. She was aware of having the option for extended time. She felt that she would not always need it, but it was a good safety net. She understood the recommendations. Very little, if anything, surprised her. A visit to her school guidance counselor during the summer with C was a good way to build a supportive relationship. However, in a large school, we did not expect constant monitoring and encouraged C to let her teachers know that she had a 504 plan.

Required accommodations such as extended time are relatively easy to implement, but not all teachers make an effort to follow instructional recommendations. We decided to advocate for C and help her teachers understand what would be most helpful for C to succeed. We did not want to be threatening or contentious. Rather, we sought to share what almost every teacher would agree are effective teaching strategies for all students. We summarized and directed the recommendations to make them most relevant to the teacher:

Does C ever seem to miss something that is going on in class? The fewer steps explained at once, the better. The more check-ins, the better.

Does C have trouble finishing in-class writing, homework assignments, or other activities? The Plan calls for 50% additional time for in-class assessments, to reduce length of written assignments (to the extent possible), and a quiet work area.

Does C have difficulty moving/transitioning from one task to another and completing work on either of the tasks? Issue a prompt or warning—probably in addition to what you already do with the kids.

Does C speak up in class? C needs to be an effective self-advocate but will need your encouragement when she asks for assistance and clarification. Sitting in the front of the classroom can help with her distractibility.

Do these recommendations make sense to you? We look forward to working together so that C has a great experience in your class.

She made the transition to ninth grade with no more bumps and bruises than any student. We had decided to be cautious and place her in an academic track instead of the honors track that her older brother had followed. As the year went on, she started to slide a bit. She seemed to lose motivation. She was doing okay but not as well as she could.

She wondered if she needed to up her dose of Ritalin. Some parents might be horrified at having their child make this suggestion, but we felt it was another example of her self-advocacy, of her wanting to find paths to success. Her doctor agreed that an increase would make sense.

But then she came to a realization that medication was not the cause of her malaise. She was bored in her undemanding academic track classes. The other students were disinterested and disengaged—and, according to C, some of the teachers were not much better. She did not want to be in this type of environment.

She began lobbying be put into honors classes in her sophomore year. We were not convinced she was ready, but we agreed that she should try. At the end of the school year, several of her teachers and the guidance counselor told us that C could make this transition.

(Continued)

(Continued)

To our delight, her sophomore year has been a positive change. C is thinking more about her future. She has connected working hard in the present with achieving long-term goals. She made us admit we had underestimated her. We had to confess that we were wrong—the ultimate victory for a teenage girl.

It would be tempting to criticize C for not paying attention. A momentary lapse may or may not be related to ADHD. We see little to gain by making this an issue. Her ability to monitor her shift of attention demonstrates good use of executive function. Moreover, her honesty allows her to self-advocate. It takes a little more patience on our part (as parents), but the dividends far outweigh the inconvenience.

Listening to text read aloud is invaluable to many struggling readers, but it is not the equivalent of the experience of reading. After we read the assignment, C then reads it on her own. This sequence helps her to develop the cognitive schema that good readers employ. It benefits other aspects of executive function. Because she knows what to expect, she is more likely to realize that she is not understanding something and will go back and reread it.

Her teacher is using a technique that is particularly useful for C. After reading assignments are completed, the students engage in close-reading activities. They tackle written discussion questions focusing on the *why*s and *how*s of the narrative and find quotes to support their responses. This process activates a much deeper level of comprehension, but it would be much less effective if C had not acquired a solid foundation before taking on the task.

C's preparedness gives her confidence not only to self-advocate but to participate actively in group discussions. In many cases, she brings with her a deeper and broader appreciation of the book. She has acquired context through our discussions; she has increased comprehension by listening and building vocabulary; she has reinforced her initial learning through reading the text herself; she has explored nuances through close reading.

She also has learned to e-mail her teachers if she is not clear on homework. She uses that clarification to complete her assignments correctly. Her teachers see this behavior as a diligent effort to succeed in school. Her self-advocacy is only as effective as the effort she puts in to her day-to-day work.

The hard work behind self-advocacy is sometimes lost on students with learning differences. If parents and teachers do not support a responsible and realistic approach, a simplistic view of self-advocacy may exacerbate learned helplessness. Children may ask for help because they are giving up; the notion that they do not need to try may become inadvertently reinforced. Eventually, teachers and parents come to see them as whiners and complainers, not effective self-advocates.

Effective self-advocacy requires building credibility. A strong work ethic flourishes from aspiring to achieve. Parents and teachers are largely responsible for planting the seed and cultivating this desire. Teachers have no problem giving extra help and attention to the hardest-working kid in the class.

Travis Frank was diagnosed with ADHD, oppositional defiance disorder, and dyslexia when he was in elementary school. He has gone on to have great success in school and is studying to become an athletic trainer. Starting in seventh grade, he realized the importance of self-advocacy. He is an amazing young man who took the initiative and courage to take charge and carry his own IEP to classes. He faced the reality that seventh graders were often not taken seriously when they stand up for themselves. He enlisted the support of an advocate. He started to gain control in a big way: He ran his own IEP meetings in high school. (It can be done!) He learned to mediate arguments among adults on his committee, a skill most of us would envy. His passionate fortitude speaks volumes:

> I sit here speaking on behalf of all Special Ed kids who have been told "You'll never do anything" or "You're not smart enough." Yes, you can and yes, you are. The only way you fail is when you stop fighting, when you give up and stop trying. You need to show that teen spirit of never knowing when to quit and say "Help me or get out of my way." To the parents, teachers, and everyone else trying to help these kids, you too must never give up and you must keep watch over the kids' progress, being ready to stop anyone trying to hurt that progress. If you fight, then we will help, and in doing so, we will one day shine through, leaving all who said "No, you can't" in our wake.

We will truly help our children and students successfully transition to adult life when we say, "Yes, we can."

References

Albom, M. (1997). *Tuesdays with Morrie: An old man, a young man, and life's greatest lessons*. New York, NY: Doubleday.

Association for Children with Learning Disabilities (ACLD). (1986, Sept/Oct). ACLD description: Specific learning disabilities. *ACLD Newsbriefs, 166,* 15

Association for Mindfulness in Education. (2013). *What is mindfulness?* Wake Forest University, The Teaching and Learning Center. Retrieved June 19, 2015, from http://tlc.wfu.edu/teaching-resources/association-mindfulness-education/

Bandura, A. (1982). Self-efficacy mechanism in human agency. *American Psychologist, 37,* 122–147.

Beauchamp, T. L., & Childress, J. (1989). *Principles of biomedical ethics* (3rd ed.). New York, NY: Oxford University Press.

Bereiter, C., & Scardamalia, M. (1987). *The psychology of written composition.* Hillsdale, NJ: Lawrence Erlbaum.

Bixler, E. (2014, December). *I am a dyslexic adult.* Speech presented at the International Dyslexia Association, Maryland Branch, Members Meeting. Retrieved June 16, 2015, from https://www.facebook.com/permalink.php?story_fbid=15206495 71524749&id=1479841302272243

Bowen, B. (2013, August 7). Blacks, Latinos confront dyslexia diagnosis gap. *New Haven Independent.* Retrieved June 21, 2015, from http://dyslexia.yale.edu/MDAI/NHIndependent.html

Bradlee, Q. (2012, September 12). *Exclusive video interview: Steven Spielberg on his dyslexia.* Retrieved June 16, 2015, from http://www.friendsofquinn.com/blog/post/exclusive-video-interview-steven-spielberg-on-his-dyslexia/235

Bradlee, Q. (2013, October 11). Conversation starters. *Friends of Quinn.* Retrieved June 13, 2015, from http://www.friendsofquinn.com/blog/post/conversation-starters/35.

Bridges, W. (2004). *Transitions: Making sense of life's changes.* New York, NY: Da Capo Press.

British Psychological Society. (2013, September 5). Mindfulness training improves attention in children. *ScienceDaily.* Retrieved June 19, 2015, from http://www.sciencedaily.com/releases/2013/09/130905202847.htm

Bureau of Labor Statistics of the U.S. Department of Labor. (2015a). *Number of jobs held, labor market activity, and earning growth among the youngest baby boomers:*

Results from a longitudinal study. Retrieved June 21, 2015, from http://www .bls.gov/news.release/pdf/nlsoy.pdf

Bureau of Labor Statistics of the U.S. Department of Labor. (2015b). *Persons with a disability: Labor force characteristics.* Retrieved June 21, 2015, from http://www .bls.gov/news.release/disabl.nr0.htm

Cannon, W. (1932). *Wisdom of the body.* New York, NY: W.W. Norton & Company.

Carnegie, D. (1936). *How to make friends and influence people.* New York, NY: Simon & Schuster.

Center for Parent Information and Resources. (2010, September). *Contents of the IEP.* Retrieved June 18, 2015, from http://www.parentcenterhub.org/repository/ iepcontents/

Chopra, D. (1994). *The seven laws of spiritual success.* San Rafael, CA: New World Library/Amber Allen Press.

Cleaver, S. (2014, September 15). Technology in the classroom: Helpful or harmful? *Education.com.* Retrieved June 17, 2015, from http://www.education.com/ magazine/article/effective-technology-teaching-child/

Cohen, S. B. (2007). *Mind reading: The interactive guide to emotions, version 1.3 with game zone, learning center, and library* [CD-ROM]. London, England: Jessica Kingsley Publishers.

Common Core State Standards Initiative. (2014). *What is not covered by the Standards.* Retrieved June 17, 2015, from http://www.corestandards.org/ELA-Literacy/ introduction/key-design-consideration/

Common Core State Standards. (2012). [website]. Retrieved June 25, 2015, from http://www.corestandards.org/

Connolly, J. (2011). *The book of lost things.* New York, NY: Simon & Schuster.

Cortiella, C., & Horowitz, S. H. (2014). *The state of learning disabilities: Facts, trends and emerging issues.* New York, NY: National Center for Learning Disabilities.

Covey, S. (1989). *The seven habits of highly effective people.* New York, NY: Free Press.

Deák, G. O. (2003). The development of cognitive flexibility and language abilities. In R. Kail (Ed.), *Advances in child development and behavior* (Vol. 31, 271–327). San Diego, CA: Academic Press.

Deshler, D. D., Schumaker, J. B., Lenz, B. K., Bulgren, J. A., Hock, M. F., Knight, J., & Ehren, B. J. (2001). Ensuring content-area learning by secondary students with learning disabilities. *Learning Disabilities Research & Practice, 16*(2), 96–108.

Deshler, D., Ellis, A., & Lenz, B. (1996). *Teaching adolescents with learning disabilities: Strategies and methods.* Denver, CO: Love.

Eide, B., & Eide, F. (2011). *The dyslexic advantage: Unlocking the hidden potential of the dyslexic brain.* New York, NY: Hudson Street Press.

Finch, D. (2012). *The journal of best practices: A memoir of marriage, Asperger Syndrome, and one man's quest to be a better husband.* New York, NY: Simon & Schuster.

Gerber, P. J., & Reiff, H. B. (1991). *Speaking for themselves: Ethnographic interviews of successful adults with learning disabilities.* Ann Arbor: University of Michigan Press.

Giddens, A. (Ed.). (1972). *Emile Durkheim: Selected writings*. Cambridge, United Kingdom: Cambridge University Press.

Gladwell, M. (2013). *David and Goliath: Underdogs, misfits, and the art of battling giants*. New York, NY: Little, Brown and Company.

Hammill, D. D. (1990). On defining learning disabilities: An emerging consensus. *Journal of Leaning Disabilities, 23*(2), 74–84.

Hart Research Associates. (2013). *It takes more than a major: Employer priorities for college learning and student success*. Retrieved June 24, 2015, from https://www .aacu.org/sites/default/files/files/LEAP/2013_EmployerSurvey.pdf

Haybron, D. (2008). *The pursuit of unhappiness: The elusive psychology of well-being*. Oxford, England: Oxford University Press.

Higher Education Opportunity Act. (2008). Retrieved June 17, 2015, from http:// www.gpo.gov/fdsys/pkg/PLAW-110publ315/html/PLAW-110publ315.htm

Holland, J. L. (1994). *The self-directed search*. Odessa, FL: Psychological Assessment Resources.

Hoy, C., Gregg, N., Wisenbaker, J., Manglitz, E., King, M., & Moreland, E. (1997). Depression and anxiety in two groups of adults with learning disabilities. *Learning Disability Quarterly, 20*, 280–291.

Individuals with Disabilities Education Improvement Act (IDEA). (2004). *Statute: Title I/A Sec. 601 short title; table of contents; findings; purposes* (numeral 5, Sections A and B). Retrieved June 18, 2015, from http://idea.ed.gov/explore/ view/p/,root,statute,I,A,601,

Johnson, D. J., & Blalock, J. W. (Eds.). (1987). *Adults with learning disabilities: Clinical studies*. Orlando, FL: Grune & Stratton.

Jones, A. (2013, September 6). Dear people who do not have child with disabilities. *No Points for Style* [web log]. Retrieved June 18, 2105, from http://www .nopointsforstyle.com/2013/08/dear-people-who-do-not-have-a-child-with-disabilities.html

Jordan, L. (n.d.). Cognitive strategies. *The University of Kansas*. Retrieved June 16, 2015, from http://www.specialconnections.ku.edu/?q=instruction/ cognitive_strategies

Kamen, L. P., & Seligman, M. E. P. (1987). Explanatory style and health. *Current Psychology, 6*(3), 207–218.

Korelitz, J. H. (2009). *Admission*. New York, NY: Grand Central Publishing.

Lauder, H. (2002, November 16). Meh. *Urbandictionary.com*. Retrieved June 19, 2015, from http://www.urbandictionary.com/define.php?term=Meh

Layard, R. (2005). *Happiness: Lessons from a new science*. New York, NY: Penguin Press.

Levinson, D. (1986). *The seasons of a man's life*. New York, NY: Ballantine Books.

Maiers, A. (2014). Increase learning by securing students' hearts. *Angelamaiers. com*. Retrieved June 8, 2015, from http://www.angelamaiers.com/2014/03/ increase-learning-by-securing-students-hearts.html

Maslow, A. (1954). *Motivation and personality*. New York, NY: Harper.

Mather, N., & Tanner, N. (2014). Introduction to the special issue: A pattern of strengths and weaknesses approach. *Learning Disabilities: A Multidisciplinary Journal, 20*(1), 1–7.

McClean, G. (2015, June 9). Disability and stress in the workplace. *About.com*. Retrieved June 13, 2015, from http://learningdisabilities.about.com/od/emotionalhealth/a/Disability-And-Stress-In-The-Workplace.htm

McLeod, S. A. (2014). Carl Rogers. *Simply Psychology*. Retrieved June 25, 2015, from http://www.simplypsychology.org/carl-rogers.html

Morgan, E., & Klein, C. (2000). *The dyslexic adult in a non-dyslexic world*. Hoboken, NJ: Wiley.

Morrison, G. M., & Cosden, M. A. (1997). Risk, resilience and adjustment of individuals with learning disabilities. *Learning Disability Quarterly, 20*(1), 43–60.

Moyer, J. (2014). *Just tell me I can't: How Jamie Moyer defied the radar gun and defeated time*. New York, NY: Grand Central Publishing.

National Joint Committee on Learning Disabilities (NJCLD). (1991). Learning disabilities: Issues on definition. *Asha, 33*(Suppl. 5), 18–20.

Newman, L., Wagner, M., Cameto, R., Knokey, A-M., & Shaver, D. (2010). *Comparisons across time of the outcomes of youth with disabilities up to 4 years after high school*. A report of findings from the National Longitudinal Transition Study (NLTS) and the National Longitudinal Transition Study-2 (NLTS2) (NCSER 2010-3008). Menlo Park, CA: SRI International.

Ofiesh, N. (2006). Response to Intervention: Why we need comprehensive evaluations as part of the process. *Psychology in the Schools, 43*(8), 883–888.

Ofiesh, N. (2010). *MASSive: A multifaceted approach to school success for individuals with learning differences*. Retrieved June 16, 2015, from http://www.nicoleofiesh.com/intervention.html

Osborne, P. (2009). *LD SAT study guide*. New York, NY: Alpha Books.

Palincsar, A. S., & Brown, A. L. (1984). Reciprocal teaching of comprehension-fostering and comprehension-monitoring activities. *Cognition and Instruction, 1*(2), 117–175.

Random House online dictionary. (2013). dis-. Retrieved June 12, 2015, from http://dictionary.reference.com/browse/dis?&o=100074&s=

Raskind, M., & Stanberry, K. (2015). *Assistive technology for kids with LD: An overview*. Retrieved April 23, 2015, from http://www.greatschools.org/gk/articles/assistive-technology-for-kids-with-learning-disabilities-an-overview/

Rathod, S. (2014). 5 subjects schools should include in curriculum. *Voniz*. Retrieved June 25, 2015, from https://www.voniz.com/articles/5-subjects-schools-include-curriculum/

Reiff, H. B., Gerber, P. J., & Ginsberg, R. (1997). *Exceeding expectations: Successful adults with learning disabilities*. Austin, TX: PRO-ED.

Roffman, A., Herzog, J., & Wershba-Gershon, P. M. (1994). Helping young adults understand their learning disabilities. *Journal of Learning Disabilities, 27*, 413–419.

Rogers, C. (1951). *Client-centered therapy: Its current practice, implications and theory*. London, England: Constable.

Rogers, C. (1959). A theory of therapy, personality and interpersonal relationships as developed in the client-centered framework. In S. Koch (Ed.), *Psychology: A study of a science*. (Vol. 3, pp. 236–257). New York, NY: McGraw-Hill.

Rogers, C. (1961). *On becoming a person: A psychotherapist's view of psychotherapy.* Boston, MA: Houghton Mifflin.

Rosenshine, B. (1997, March 24–28). *The case for explicit, teacher-led, cognitive strategy instruction.* Paper presented at the annual meeting of the American Educational Research Association in Chicago, IL. Retrieved June 16, 2015, from http:// www.formapex.com/telechargementpublic/rosenshine1997a.pdf?616d13afc 6835dd26137b409becc9f87=4d34101224fa8bcc8a53050fda55c277

Roy, R. (1989, March 20). Check mates. *Fairfield County Advocate.*

Scholz, M., Niesch, H., Steffen, O., Ernst, B., Loeffler, M., Witruk, E., & Schwarz, H. (2008). Impact of chess training on mathematics performance and concentration ability of children with learning disabilities. *International Journal of Special Education, 23,* 138–148.

Spekman, N. J., Goldberg, R. J., & Herman, K. L. (1993). An exploration of risk and resilience in the lives of individuals with learning disabilities. *Learning Disabilities Research & Practice, 8*(1), 11–18.

Stossel, S. (2014). *My age of anxiety: Fear, hope, dread, and the search for peace of mind.* New York, NY: Knopf.

U.S. Department of Justice, Civil Rights Division. (2009). *Disability rights section: A guide to disability rights laws.* Retrieved June 21, 2015, from http://www.ada .gov/cguide.htm

U.S. Office of Education. (1977). *Definition and criteria for defining students as learning disabled.* Federal Register, 42:250, p. 65083. Washington, DC: U.S. Government Printing Office.

Van Reusen, A. K., Bos, C. S., Schumaker, J. B., & Deshler, D. D. (2007). *The self-advocacy strategy.* Lawrence, KS: Edge Enterprises.

Van Reusen, A. K., Bos, S., Schumaker, J. B., & Deshler, D. D. (2007). Self-Advocacy strategy. *Strategic Instruction Model (SIM).* Lawrence, KS: Edge Enterprises.

Welkes, T. (2008). *Barron's SAT strategies for students with learning disabilities.* Hauppauge, NY: Barron's Educational Series.

West, T. (2009). *In the mind's eye: Creative visual thinkers, gifted dyslexics, and the rise of visual technologies.* New York, NY: Prometheus Books.

Index

A SAGE Company

CORWIN HAS ONE MISSION: to enhance education through intentional professional learning.

We build long-term relationships with our authors, educators, clients, and associations who partner with us to develop and continuously improve the best evidence-based practices that establish and support lifelong learning.

Solutions you want. Experts you trust. Results you need.